Rescue Skills is the fruit of years of co[...]
who are skilled at their craft, offer robust, practical wisdom that flows from
biblical truths and pastoral hearts. *Rescue Skills* serves as an invaluable guide,
not only for helping those struggling with porn in particular, but also for
bearing one another's burdens in general. I highly recommend this book
for any disciple and disciple-maker.

—**Robert K. Cheong**, Pastor of Care and Counseling, Sojourn
Community Church, Louisville, Kentucky

Brothers and sisters! This book has the potential to not only change the way
you offer ministry to women and men who battle sexual sin but to transform churches. Imagine what would happen if the body of Christ actively
engaged in personal study of the gospel with a view toward application in
discipleship to those bound up in sexual sin? Envision with me what would
happen if the church embraced practical, on-the-ground ministry rather
than merely talking about sexuality. *Rescue Skills* can powerfully encourage
and equip you through the guidance of two experienced pastors who have
written this book from years in the trenches of loving people.

—**Ellen Mary Dykas**, Women's Ministry Director, Harvest USA;
Author, *Toxic Relationships: Taking Refuge in Christ*

This is a hard book to endorse—there are just too many good things to say!
Holmes and Reju know the questions the helper must ask, the excuses the
struggler will offer, the inner struggles that define the porn user's world,
the way to help that will actually make a difference. *Rescue Skills* somehow manages to teach compassion for those who dive into porn without
being soft on their sin. It also brings refreshingly novel topics to the battle,
including reviving the conscience, taking your body's struggle seriously,
and appreciating rather than avoiding true beauty. *Rescue Skills* is the most
realistic yet hope-filled book I've read on helping people with pornography.

—**Alasdair Groves**, Executive Director, Christian Counseling &
Educational Foundation

Compassionate, fresh, practical, convicting, and reproducible, *Rescue Skills*
is the right book at the right time for those who are facing sexual brokenness

and the loved ones who are seeking to help them. Within these pages lies the aggregate wisdom of two pastor-practitioners—counseling leaders who have dedicated their lives to the skill and beauty of helping people to experience gospel liberation. Whether you are personally fighting for freedom or counseling those under attack, this book forms a new weapon in the arsenal to help win the war.

—**Dave Harvey**, President, Great Commission Collective; Author, *I Still Do: Growing Closer and Stronger through Life's Defining Moments*

Reju and Holmes give us page after page of wisdom—God's truth applied in practical ways to a widespread problem that all counselors and disciplers face. It is gospel-infused, biblically driven, and church-based, yet filled with concrete steps and sprinkled with case examples from their counseling ministries. A rich, readable resource for every Christian who wants to help friends who are tempted by or enslaved to pornography.

—**Robert D. Jones**, Associate Pastor of Biblical Counseling, The Southern Baptist Theological Seminary; Author, *Uprooting Anger: Biblical Help for a Common Problem*

In *Rescue Skills*, Deepak and Jonathan set out to help counselors to become better helpers and disciplers of men or women struggling with addiction, and this book certainly accomplishes that task. Each chapter is filled with solid, practical guidance that can be put into practice immediately—guidance that is consistently rooted in God's Word. This book is the perfect companion to *Rescue Plan*!

—**Kristin L. Kellen**, Assistant Professor of Biblical Counseling, Southeastern Baptist Theological Seminary

The sin of pornography is a growing issue in the church. Knowing how to help someone in this situation can be daunting. *Rescue Skills* is a gift to the church. Biblical counselors Deepak Reju and Jonathan Holmes have meticulously written a biblical roadmap for those who are coming alongside someone who struggles with pornography.

Rescue Skills translates biblical theology into practice through the process of biblical discipleship. It teaches the reader how to grow in essential skills, such as listening, asking heart-probing questions, and executing a biblical plan of action to give help and hope to the sexually broken.

The easy-to-read chapters illustrate real-life narratives and provide immediate guidance in how to navigate difficult conversations. The reader is encouraged to practice the skills right away by using the application questions and reflections at the end of each chapter.

This book is for church leaders and anyone who knows someone who is struggling with pornography. The reader will gain insight, wisdom, and encouragement to grow in their personal skills to be a better minister and friend to the sexually broken. I highly recommend this book!
—**Shannon McCoy**, Biblical Counseling Director, Valley Center
   Community Church, Valley Center, California

Read this book and you will be better equipped to help those who are struggling with pornography. In short and practically applied chapters full of true-to-life examples, Deepak Reju and Jonathan Holmes have provided a highly useable resource for anyone who wants to help someone to escape from an addiction to porn. Refreshingly honest, biblically faithful, deeply realistic, and filled with the hope that only grace can bring, this is a book that pastors, counsellors, and friends will turn to again and again.
—**Steve Midgley**, Executive Director, Biblical Counselling UK; Senior
   Minister, Christ Church, Cambridge

Rescue Skills offers the most comprehensive approach of any resource I have seen to equip counselors to offer wise, practical, biblical advice to people who indulge in pornography and other sexual sins. The authors are very specific and real about these struggles without being salacious. They strike an appropriate balance between addressing the heart and taking action to restrain the flesh. While the book specifically addresses sexual issues, most of its wisdom would apply to helping counselees with other besetting sins. My students and counselees will benefit from this resource.
—**Jim Newheiser**, Director of the Christian Counseling Program
   and Associate Professor of Pastoral Theology, Reformed Theological
   Seminary, Charlotte; Executive Director, The Institute for Biblical
   Counseling and Discipleship

The scope of the church's porn problem is staggering. It's no wonder that the world mocks us as the porn industry seeks relentlessly to prove that Christ is a cuckold. We need many more disciplers equipped to lead strugglers away from sexual sin and into the gracious arms of Jesus. This book is a stockpile of necessary wisdom. As you read it, your arsenal will be filled with multidimensional tactics specific to the battle against porn. You will come away prepared to be a better friend, spouse, counselor, or pastor to the many men and women who desperately need wise care.

—**Jenny and Curtis Solomon**, Cofounders, Solomon SoulCare;
    Authors, *Reclaim Your Marriage: Grace for Wives Who Have Been Hurt by Pornography* and *Redeem Your Marriage: Hope for Husbands Who Have Hurt through Pornography*

No other book I've read more clearly teaches churches the practical skills necessary to help those who are struggling with sexual sin. *Rescue Skills* is rich with stories that clarify how to wisely help both men and women. But it's not just a catalogue of biblical precision tools. Most of all, it is the merciful heart of our ultimate Rescuer, Jesus Christ, that is on display. Each page displays his gentle heart toward sinners, providing hope and motivation to the reader. This will be an indispensable resource for our church's counseling team going forward.

—**Tim St. John**, Associate Pastor, Lighthouse Community Church,
    Torrance, California

What happens when two seasoned shepherds team up to write a guide to help us to disciple those who struggle to overcome sexual sin? We receive the hope-infused, grace-fueled, Christ-centered, and biblically faithful tool you hold in your hands. *Rescue Skills* is a gift to all who are motivated by love to come alongside others to carefully discern how to help them to get to the roots of their struggle, so that they may experience lasting transformation. This wisely crafted instrument, in the hands of gracious disciplers, is sure to help many to learn to walk in the victory of gospel-rooted obedience.

—**Paul Tautges**, Author, *Anxiety: Knowing God's Peace*; Senior Pastor,
    Cornerstone Community Church, Mayfield Heights, Ohio; Founder,
    Counseling One Another

Walking alongside people who are sexually broken can feel like a daunting task—their actions can confuse us; their underlying heart struggles can be hard to address. Within these pages, however, there is hope and help. Whether you are a formal counselor or an individual who wants to spur on a friend, *Rescue Skills* is packed full of biblical nourishment, methodological wisdom, and a wealth of encouragement to keep nurturing our own hearts as we help those around us. Accessible, practical, and dripping with grace—it's a book I'll undoubtedly be coming back to time and again.

—**Helen Thorne**, Director of Training and Resources, Biblical
    Counselling UK

Rescue Skills is a delightful combination of sound theology and practical instruction on how to improve our actual counseling methodology. Jonathan and Deepak are a special blessing to Christ's church because they are immersed in biblical truth and experienced in helping people with real-life struggles. This book will help you to grow in your understanding of the process of counseling. The gospel is the greatest rescue project ever. May our Redeemer help us to become more skilled in this life-giving and life-changing endeavor.

—**Steve Viars**, Pastor, Faith Church, Lafayette, Indiana; Author,
    *Overcoming Bitterness: Moving from Life's Greatest Hurts to a Life Filled
    with Joy*

Rescue Skills is an essential go-to for every pastor, church leader, small-group leader, caring friend, mentor, or counselor who desires to grow in their people-helping skills. And that's all of us. You will find this book incredibly helpful as you minister to people with a variety of struggles, not just the sexually broken. Developing and honing the art of wise caring takes time, patience, and practice. You will probably read this book with one specific person or situation in mind, but I think you will come back to it again and again to grow in proficiency as other needs arise. I recommend keeping *Rescue Skills*, and its companion volume, *Rescue Plan*, close at hand.

—**Greg Wilson**, Licensed Professional Counselor and Supervisor, Soul
    Care Associates; Coauthor, *When Home Hurts: A Guide for Responding
    Wisely to Domestic Abuse in Your Church*

RESCUE SKILLS

RESCUE SKILLS

ESSENTIAL SKILLS FOR
RESTORING
THE SEXUALLY BROKEN

DEEPAK REJU & JONATHAN D. HOLMES

P&R PUBLISHING
P.O. BOX 817 • PHILLIPSBURG • NEW JERSEY 08865-0817

Library of Congress Cataloging-in-Publication Data

Names: Reju, Deepak, 1969- author. | Holmes, Jonathan D., author.
Title: Rescue skills : essential skills for restoring the sexually broken / Deepak Reju, Jonathan D. Holmes.
Description: Phillipsburg, New Jersey : P&R Publishing, [2021] | Includes bibliographical references. | Summary: "Looking to help someone who struggles with pornography? This book provides a trove of biblical strategies developed out of years of counseling experience-and you can use them right away"-- Provided by publisher.
Identifiers: LCCN 2021027947 | ISBN 9781629959054 (paperback) | ISBN 9781629959061 (epub)
Subjects: LCSH: Pornography--Religious aspects--Christianity. | Sex--Religious aspects--Christianity. | Pastoral counseling. | Peer counseling in the church. | Counseling--Religious aspects--Christianity.
Classification: LCC BV4597.6 .R45355 2021 | DDC 241/.667--dc23
LC record available at https://lccn.loc.gov/2021027947

To our dear wives, Sarah and Jennifer,
who have stood beside us through thick and thin,
good times and bad.
Thank you for your love, patience and grace . . .
and for putting up with our many faults!

CONTENTS

INTRODUCTION:
DO YOU HAVE WHAT IT TAKES?

MASTERS OF THEIR CRAFTS AT WORK

If you ever see gifted lawyers in a courtroom, you'll notice that they ask precise questions, follow careful lines of thinking, apply pressure at just the right moments, object when other lawyers are getting out ahead, and make persuasive speeches to the jury.

If you ever witness talented chefs in the kitchen, you'll see their creative use of ingredients, their mastery of the mechanics of making quality dough, their artistry in decorating a cake, and their expert use of kitchen tools and appliances to produce fresh pasta, sumptuous turkey, or delicious pie.

If you ever watch carpenters at work, you'll see them operating table saws and wood chisels, using nail guns, polishing and finishing the wood, and carving items with pinpoint precision and delicacy.

What do they have in common? Skills—the abilities they've learned and practiced in order to be good at their crafts. Taking the time to train and hone these necessary skills makes all the difference between an amateur and a world-class master.

If you're reading this book, you're in pursuit of skills that have eternal significance. You're an ambassador for Christ (see 2 Cor. 5:20) and a soldier in God's army (see Eph. 6:10–20). There is a war being waged for a believer's soul (see 1 Peter 2:11)—the soul of your friend who is struggling with pornography and masturbation. You want to know how to hone your skills so you can help in this war.

9

SATURDAY AFTERNOON AT A COFFEE SHOP

Imagine Tommy or Teresa meets up with you for a latte. You're sitting at the corner table of your local coffee shop. Tommy starts in: "My wife caught me looking at pornography last night. She's really mad, and I'm ashamed to even admit this to you." Or Teresa tells you, "I've been meaning to tell you this for a while—I'm really struggling. I've been reading erotic literature for the last two years, and a few months ago I started dabbling in pornography. Now it's overwhelming my life."

What do you say? How do you respond? Where do you go in the Bible? What questions do you ask? How do you probe his conscience? How do you help her with her guilt and shame? There are a thousand questions you could ask—and a thousand and one things you could do in response. But what's best and wisest for *this* moment and for *this* specific person?

If you're like most Christians, you're not sure what to say or do. When it comes to a conversation with a friend who is struggling sexually, the stakes are high. You're at the front lines of the battle against temptation. Don't be afraid! There is much you can do.

This is where we come in. We want to help you.

The art of loving wisely draws on many skills. Asking a good question. Probing a person's shame. Pressing hard at the right moment. Applying Scripture thoughtfully and lovingly. Inspiring hope and instilling a Christ-centered identity. Being sensitive to his conscience. These are just a few of the skills you need. This book will help you to develop and hone these skills to help people who are struggling with pornography.

We've written *Rescue Skills* for the helper and discipler—the person who sits in the trenches with a struggling friend. Our target audience is pastors, counselors, best friends, parents, small-group leaders, roommates, fellow church members, and really anyone who is coming alongside a friend who struggles with pornography. If you are a believer who is committed to fighting against sin, striving for faith, modeling Christlikeness, and providing hope, this book is for you.

If you're personally overrun with pornography, you're welcome to read this book. You'll get plenty out of it. You can also check out our resources list in the back to find books written specifically for you.

A quick note on the use of pronouns: We understand that porn addiction is a problem for both men and women, so we use both masculine and feminine pronouns throughout this book. Much of the content applies to both men and women, regardless of the specific pronoun we have chosen for a given section.

A CHALLENGE TO GROW IN YOUR SKILLS

As you read the pages ahead, our hope is not just that you will grow in head knowledge but that you will work at becoming better at helping and discipling others. You're an ambassador for the Lord Jesus to a friend who is sexually addicted. This book can help you to grow in asking thoughtful questions, probing the heart, ministering to guilt and shame, encouraging the weary, and so much more. Don't wait until you have read to the end. With each chapter, start practicing the skills right away. Make use of them in your very next conversation.

At the end of each chapter, there are reflection questions for you (the discipler) to consider and a practical step for you and your friend to take in the fight against sexual sin. Make use of these two bits of application. You'll get *much more* from this book if you do the application. Don't read to fill up your head. Show in what you do that faith plus action is the best combination (see James 2:20–23).

Keep in mind that no one likes to be a project. If your friend thinks you've turned him into a class assignment, that's a quick way to sour the relationship. If you show that you love him and are committed over the long run to his spiritual good, now *that's* the recipe for success. We're much more inclined to listen to someone who we know loves us and is acting for our good.

God is working in your friend's life (see Phil. 2:13). The Spirit brings conviction and instills hope in desperate situations. Yet God uses means—like you, a loving friend—to accomplish his purposes (see 2 Cor. 5:18; Gal. 6:1). He uses you to talk, pray, ask questions, comfort, exhort, love, support, encourage, and do so many other things.

Are you ready to begin? Let's start with a few important reminders on what we're dealing with.

FOUNDATIONAL INFORMATION
FROM *RESCUE PLAN*

This book is a companion to *Rescue Plan: Charting a Course to Restore Prisoners of Pornography*. Ideally you will read both books, since *Rescue Plan*

- lays important theological groundwork about porn addictions
- gives extensive help for understanding and battling the sin of masturbation
- explains how sexual struggles are similar and different for men and women
- shows how to counsel people with a variety of unique needs (teenagers, singles, those who are dating, married people)

Even if you're more interested in the skills than the plan, don't skip these important notes! They are the foundation for what lies ahead.

Although porn strugglers may not think of themselves as addicts, addiction marks their behavior. To help them, you need to understand the nature of addiction and the factors that make them most likely to act impulsively when they are tempted.

GOD'S VIEW OF ADDICTIONS

Our culture has a lot to say about what an addict is and is not. We want to be careful at the outset to think about addictions according to the Bible. After all, we're Christians—so we want God's Word to define how we think about everything, including porn addictions. On the pages of Scripture are five concepts—voluntary slavery, double-mindedness, foolishness, idolatry, and disordered desires—that come alive as we describe the nature of addictions.

Voluntary Slavery

Samir makes a choice to sin—to look at pornography. It's just one time, but it awakens in him an appetite for more. After his guilt and shame over violating his conscience dissipates, Samir chooses to do it again, and again, and again. His body and heart crave more, the cravings grow and take over his life, and one day Samir ends up enslaved. One dumb choice leads to death, not life. One titillating moment leads to months of bondage to sexual sin.

Double-Mindedness

Jillian hates her sin and loves it. She fantasizes about having sex and reads erotic literature. She hates her sin the moment after the guilt and shame kick in. However, give it time, and the cravings resurface, her loneliness feels fierce, her heart longs again, and her body wants more. Her affections for the addiction show themselves again. In one breath she says, "I've got to stop," and, in the very next, "I want more! I deserve more!"

Foolishness

Addiction is marked by foolishness, which is described vividly throughout the book of Proverbs. Take Javier's case, for example. He's been hooked on porn and masturbation for five years. The sin has overtaken his life. He sleeps very little so he can get yet another fix. He goes to church, but he spurns wisdom, insight, and a godly life (see Prov. 1:7). His friends talk to him, but he's not open to correction (see 12:1); rather, he feels justified in his own mind that he is right (see 12:15). "You guys don't get what I've been going through," he thinks. He despises the good sense in his pastor's and best friend's words (see 23:9). He lacks sense (see 8:5). He's hasty (see 29:20), and he's prone to quarreling (see 20:3). His parents are at a loss as to what to do. If given a chance, Javier will wound loved ones and friends (see 26:10). He will not turn from his evil desires (see 13:19). He returns to his porn and often repeats his porn-use habits, like a dog returning to its vomit (see 26:11).

Idolatry

An idol is anything strugglers worship over and above God (see Rom. 1:25). In the twenty-first century, they don't bow down to an idol in an Old Testament temple. The issue goes much deeper. There are idols at war in their hearts (see Ezek. 14:1–5), promising them power, adventure, affirmation, control, pleasure, recognition, significance, and happiness. Leah looks at porn, fantasizes, and masturbates because she wants to be loved and to have sex. Her idols are the gods of relationship ("I want a man") and experience ("I want to be intimate"). She can't get what she wants in the real world, so she makes up a fantasy world to get what she wants.

Disordered Desires

The addicted heart has passions, desires, and cravings (see James 1:14–15; 4:1) that are more worldly than godly. God cherishes holiness and love; the addict uses others for his own selfish gain. God teaches us to be servant-hearted and patient; porn shapes the addict to be greedy and to get his desires satisfied. If a struggler is hungry for pleasure, he'll go online and find pornographic images or videos. If he wants affirmation, he'll find someone who will give it to him. If he wants a burger, he'll drive down to McDonald's. His behavior is ruled by his disordered cravings and desires. A love for true beauty—for what God loves—becomes secondary to the carnal cravings of an addict's heart.

THE FOUR INGREDIENTS OF GIVING IN TO TEMPTATION (THE 4 A'S)

Imagine Samir or Leah sitting in his or her bedroom at 11:32 on a Friday night. It's been a hard day at work—high-pressure deadlines and a mean boss. Dating prospects and hopes for marriage are waning. As is typical, around 11 o'clock, self-pity starts to kick in, and by 11:45 the rationalizations begin: "God doesn't care." "You deserve something for your troubles." "It doesn't matter, God will forgive you."

What makes Samir or Leah act out in the moment? There are four active ingredients at work when an addict feels tempted and pursues porn—access, anonymity, appetite, and atheism.[1] The Four *A*s. Take any one of these away and the act of looking at porn becomes harder.

Access

Long gone are the days when a man walked away from a newsstand with a pornographic magazine in a brown bag or walked into an adult store to buy a VHS or DVD. With the emergence of the Internet, everything has changed. For one thing, the Internet lowered the barrier of entry for women. The playing field has evened. Both men and women have free and open access to as much pornographic content as their hearts desire.

In the age of the Internet, access to online content is available virtually everywhere. That's a problem for addicts. Open access is dangerous for an addict's soul. An addict often can't resist giving in to the temptation. A phone with unlimited and unfettered access to the Internet is like a grenade in her pocket. If she's not careful, it will eventually explode.

The Internet does great good, but it also leads to great harm.

Anonymity

Addicts typically don't look at porn in a busy workroom or on the subway. They look at it alone, in their apartments, behind closed doors. They do it when no one else can see what they are doing.

Appetite

If an addict's idolatrous heart can secure access and anonymity, it satisfies his cravings and desires for more porn. Think of his sinful flesh as a dragon. If he feeds it, it never becomes satisfied. It just wants more. Idolatry and disordered desires overrun a believer. His carnal cravings dethrone God and everything else in his life. Another way to describe addictions is as *desires that run amok.*

Atheism

Satan's goal is to get a struggler to doubt God's goodness and his love, just as he did with Adam and Eve. *Did God really say . . . ? Does God really love you? Will God really follow through?* If the devil can sow the seeds of doubt, he creates a momentary atheist. When an addict listens to Satan, she turns her back on God (see Ps. 14:1), and, not surprisingly, she'll fall back into looking at porn. She gives in to her battle with unbelief, even for just thirty seconds, because she's been fooled by sin yet again. Sin always overpromises and underdelivers.

PART 1

HELPER SKILLS

To be effective in your love for your struggling friend, you'll need to grow in your skills as a discipler. Part 1 details important skills for you to master as a helper.

1

LISTENING WITH AN ACTIVE EAR

Being heard is so close to being loved that for
the average person they are almost indistinguishable.
—*David Augsburger,* Caring Enough to Hear and Be Heard

Know this, my beloved brothers and sisters:
let every person be quick to hear, slow to speak, slow to anger.
—*James 1:19*

"Hi, you're on the phone with Dr. Frasier Crane, and *I'm listening.*"
This was the memorable line that Kelsey Grammar's psychiatrist
character famously said when callers phoned in to his radio show.
Unfortunately, for the majority of Frasier's callers, Frasier was doing
anything but listening. From pestering his radio producer to occu-
pying himself with his own troubles, Frasier's listening was a bit of
a sham.

Oftentimes we can be guilty of the same practice in our care
and discipleship. A lot of nods and shakes of the head may seem to
communicate that we are listening, but our minds are far from the
people in front of us. We ask a question, only to formulate an answer
to what we *think* will be the response. We offer answers to problems
that show we have not fully tried to understand the struggler's world.
Or we interrupt strugglers mid-sentence, showing that what we say
is more important to us than their comments.

The fact that people struggle to listen is nothing new. The word
listen is used over fifteen hundred times in the Bible, and more often

than not the issue is that people do not listen.[1] The skill of listening is something we all can grow in. When you listen to others, remember that more is happening than the mere auditory reception of words.

WHO IS YOUR LISTENING ROLE MODEL?

Why do we listen? We listen because God listens to us. We mirror God when we pause and listen to others.

> But truly God has listened;
> > he has attended to the voice of my prayer. (Ps. 66:19)

> I love the LORD, because he has heard
> > my voice and my pleas for mercy.
> Because he inclined his ear to me,
> > therefore I will call on him as long as I live. (Ps. 116:1–2)

Or think about how Christ carefully listens. For example, in John 4, a Samaritan woman comes to Jacob's well to get water at midday. They talk about living water, her sexual sin, and the need to worship in Spirit and truth. Christ hears her when she speaks to her deepest needs (for a Savior) and her greatest shame (sexual sin with multiple men). He listens to all of it—her misunderstandings, her shame, her theological inquiries, and much more. And he responds with gentleness, honesty, theological truth, and love.

In addition to imitating Christ (who is the *best* of all listeners), there are many good reasons why a Christian *should* carefully listen. We pay attention to struggling believers because it helps us to understand their troubles. As we listen, we build more comprehensive pictures of these people's lives. We take note of their desires, frustrations, and suffering, because doing so communicates love and concern and models grace and patience.

The stark contrast is the proverbial fool. The fool is the epitome of a *horrible* listener.

A fool takes no pleasure in understanding,
    but only in expressing his opinion. (Prov. 18:2)

If one gives an answer before he hears,
    it is his folly and shame. (Prov. 18:13)

Do you see a man who is hasty in his words?
    There is more hope for a fool than for him. (Prov. 29:20)

The biblical picture of the fool is one who doesn't listen and understand but speaks too quickly. He is impulsive. He answers before he hears. He doesn't take the time to hear and then speak. In Proverbs 18:2, the fool finds pleasure *only* in saying what he wants to say. In verse 13, because of his impulsive speech that lacks understanding, he is deemed foolish and shameful. Or, as one commentator put it, "stupid and a disgrace."[2]

Who are you more like when it comes to listening—Christ or the fool? Are you good at it, or are you lazy and driven by your agenda? Do you struggle to listen well? Or are you humble enough to admit you are a poor listener?

WHAT KIND OF LISTENER ARE YOU— GOOD, BAD, OR MEDIOCRE?

It's clear—listening is both difficult and Christlike. How good or bad of a listener are you? Take the listening test—rate yourself on a scale of one to ten. *One* is the worst listener on the planet. *Ten* is the best listener in the entire universe. Take a moment, get a number in your mind, and then write it down below.

Rate yourself: I am _____ out of 10.

Here's what to do with this number: Go and talk with someone who knows you really well. Ask her to rate you as a listener, and get her to explain *why* she ranked you the way she did. For example, you

23

self-identify as an 8, but your spouse or parent or best friend says you are a 3. You're surprised. So you ask, "I ranked myself as an 8, but you gave me a 3. Why did you rank me that low?" Be humble enough to hear her explanation. If you hear and own what she is saying, you'll grow as a listener. We promise. But don't ask for help if you are *not* humble enough to receive feedback and make adjustments.

"True listening wars against the entrenched selfishness of the human heart. The listening heart is one that seeks to give, to learn, to welcome, to serve. In a small but real way, listening imitates the self-emptying act of Jesus, who voluntarily released his claims on ruling in order to serve and give his life. The listening heart strives to put away control, all the ways we can manipulate a conversation for our gain. It is able to stop in the middle of a thought and say, 'You're right.' . . . The listening heart seeks to be present, to be focused on something other than itself and to give its attention away."
—**Adam McHugh**[3]

Now imagine Andy comes to you after several years of struggle and tells you his story. He's watching pornography two or three times a day. He's got access through his smartphone and has not locked it down by using available restrictions. He broke up with his girlfriend recently, and, to mask the pain, he has plunged into pornography more than ever. He's broken over his sin but also blind to a lot of foolish mistakes he's making. He's got too much access, and you know you need to help him to build restrictions into his phone and to build self-discipline in his thought life.

Here's the kicker, though—as you meet with Andy for lunch, he tells you his story for fifty minutes nonstop. No breathers. No pauses. He just keeps talking *at* you, not *with* you. How would you do in listening to him? At the forty-fifth minute, would your mind be wandering, or could you stick with it? Would you keep listening as diligently as you did in the first few minutes? Rate yourself again on the same scale as before: *one* (worst listener) to *ten* (best listener).

Rate yourself: After forty-five minutes of listening to Andy, I would rate myself _____ out of 10.

Listening is hard work, especially the longer the conversation goes. Are you willing to do the hard work?

WHAT SHOULD YOU LISTEN FOR?

With that being said, what should we be listening for? What can we tune our ears toward? Let's take the Four *As* and see where we need to pay special attention.

Access
- Where does he access his pornography?
- What excuses does she give for leaving outlets for pornography unprotected and unaccountable?
- When you offer accountability measures as a way toward purity, does he offer half-hearted rationalizations? How does he justify his sin?

Anonymity
- Who is mentioned in his story? Who are the key people in his life?
- How connected or isolated is she? Who knows what is going on in her life?
- Has he ever disclosed this struggle to someone other than you? If so, what was the result?
- How long has she struggled with pornography without telling anyone?
- Has he realized that pornography isolates him from people?

Our friend Don says things like "I'm alone," or "No one cares," or "God has abandoned me." This communicates his isolation.

A fellow church member, Gina, says, "I don't need help" or "I can do it on my own." Her deliberate pursuit of anonymity tells us she is prideful and foolish, as no one can survive on her own in a fight against sexual sin.

Appetite

- How does she describe the drive toward pornography?
- Does he recognize the desires that ensnare his heart? Or is he ignorant of the war in his heart?
- Has she done any heart-level work to understand what happens within her in moments of temptation?

Listen for words that communicate her cravings—*want, desire, need, must have, look forward to, can't go without,* and so on.

Atheism

- Does she ever mention God in her struggle? Or does she leave him completely out of it?
- What's his functional view of God?
- Does she believe that God cares about her and her situation?
- Does he think God can change him? Or has he given up on God?
- What other doubts does she express about God?

Listening well involves asking questions and then sifting through answers. The answers are critical because they inform how you move forward. What would happen if a doctor began an operation without taking time to ask questions and listen for the answers? Such a dynamic could lead to serious injury and malpractice. The same holds true for us if we do not listen well. We can offer ill-timed advice or biblically misleading counsel when we fail to listen first.

Every time people speak to us, they are bearing witness and testimony to what is in their hearts (see Prov. 4:23; Luke 6:43–45). Therefore, every piece of content we hear is important, though some details and pieces of information may be *less* important than others. God knows that listening is something we struggle with, which is why he admonishes us to "be quick to hear, slow to speak, slow to anger" (James 1:19). It's commonly observed that God created us with one mouth and two ears. He did that to remind us of the ratio of speaking to listening that we are to engage in.

A *confessional* view of God is an understanding of who God is according to how he reveals himself in his Word. A *functional* view of God is what we think about God, but it's rooted in assumptions and beliefs that are based on education, experience, or worldly wisdom rather than God's Word. For example, Hector knows the Bible says God loves him, but Hector's functional view of God is that the Lord doesn't love him, maybe even dislikes him, because Hector hasn't overcome his addiction.

PRACTICAL SKILLS WHEN LISTENING

Here are a few additional ways you can demonstrate love as you listen to others tell their stories.

Listen with your posture. Are you attentive? Do you have attentive body language—an open and relational posture rather than a closed one? Squarely face the other person. Lean in and show interest with your body language. Do not become preoccupied with other things, such as taking notes, checking your phone, or looking at the clock.

Listen with your eyes. Maintain eye contact. Look the other person in the eyes. This shows that you are engaged with him.

Listen with your mind. Are you focused on the other person, or do you zone out? Are you easily distracted?

Look for breaks in eye contact. Sometimes a break in eye contact communicates shame or guilt. The last time that I (Jonathan) talked to a struggler, I asked him to look up at me, and he said he couldn't: "I'm too ashamed of what I've done."

Pay attention to nonverbal communication. How does the other person present to you—anxious, angry, ashamed, disappointed? Can you see this in her body posture or her facial expressions? Is she folding her hands across her chest, or is she curled up in her seat? Does she appear dejected or despairing? Does she seem fidgety?

Reflect: How well do you listen, and how can you grow in this area? What can you do in your next conversation to get better? For example, should you put your cell phone out of reach so you don't get distracted?

Act: After your next meeting, talk about how you and your friend did at listening to each other. In Christ, with humility and love, give each other feedback and help each other to grow.

2

TARGETING THE HEART

*Sin isn't only doing bad things; it's more fundamentally
making good things into ultimate things. Sin is building
your life and meaning on anything, even a very good thing,
more than on God. Whatever we build our life on will
drive us and enslave us. Sin is primarily idolatry.*
—*Tim Keller, "How to Talk about Sin in a Postmodern Age"*

Keep your heart with all vigilance, for from it flow the springs of life.
—*Proverbs 4:23*

It's hard for us to get to know people and build deeper friendships because far too many of us dwell more comfortably at a superficial level of conversation. We're scared to give others access to the deep recesses of our lives. We're fearful to open up and expose ourselves. How do we move beyond the superficial and really get to know people? We cut through the surface layers and take aim at their hearts.

Walter sits across from you. He's been talking with you about his life—his job, his kids, and the basketball game last Saturday. Normal chitchat. You've talked a lot, getting caught up with his life. However, if we were handed a video of your conversation, as counseling pastors we'd tell you that Walter has been hiding from you. He's told you a lot about *his life*, but he hasn't told you about *himself*. What do we mean by that? He's hidden behind the circumstances of his life. He's talked about what's happening in his life (job, kids, basketball), but he hasn't said a thing about how he's doing. He hasn't told you about the war raging in his heart.

Typical friendly banter talks about circumstances: How's your job? Do you still like your boss? What did you do this weekend? Can you believe the Lakers beat the Knicks in Saturday's basketball game? But to really get to know someone, you've got to step beyond the circumstances, get behind the curtain, and look at his heart.

One way to do this is to ask questions that take aim at the deeper matters of the heart. If we were sitting across from Walter, we'd ask, "What really matters to you?" "What makes you tick?" "If I were to get into your mind and heart, what would I see you really worshipping?" "What does your life revolve around?" "What are your hopes, dreams, and goals?" "What motivates you to get out of bed?"

And guess what? Walter would look startled. Who talks like that? No one. Far too few people have deep conversations that move beyond superficial circumstances. Our questions press into Walter's heart. We want to know the *real* Walter—what he loves and hates; what he really worships; what really matters to him. Our questions are meant to be intrusive. They are directed at his inner person—his heart and mind. If we want deeper relationships, we should be willing to ask these kinds of questions so that we can get to know people better. And if that's not the way we normally talk, people will be really surprised.

Most of us live in terminally superficial relationships and don't know what it means to get beyond the superficial. As we get to know porn strugglers, get involved in their lives, and even help them to pursue change, it becomes vital for us to understand the biblical concept of the heart. If we address only the superficial details and circumstances of their lives but don't dig down to the depths of their hearts, our counsel falls short of what the Bible commends. To really help people, we've got to uncover and expose their hearts.

THREE PRINCIPLES OF THE HEART

The scope of this chapter does not allow us to develop a robust theology of the heart. For that we would commend to you several resources that tackle this topic in a balanced and biblical manner.[1] Still, we want to lay out three key principles regarding the heart that should guide our counseling, whether we're dealing with pornography strugglers or anyone else.

The Heart Is the Core of Who We Are

In several places in Scripture, the Hebrew or Greek words for *heart* describe "being at the center of something" (see, for example, Jonah 2:3; Matt. 12:40). The heart is the core of who we are and the command center of our lives. Think of Jesus's words in Matthew 12:34, where he says, "Out of the overflow of the heart, the mouth speaks" (BSB; see also Luke 6:45) We might say, "Out of the overflow of the heart, we think, speak, act, feel, and do."

Throughout Scripture, we are told many aspects of what the heart can do:

- *Positive*: The heart can think, remember, know, discern, see, meditate, grieve, love, give, turn, pray, rejoice, sing, be faithful, be upright, seek God, repent, and believe.
- *Negative*: The heart can fear, hate, lust, become proud, deceive, set up idols, and become hardened toward God and others.

Christians understand that the heart is the "real" you. It is the essential core of who you are. Solomon writes, "As water reflects the face, so the heart reflects the true man" (Prov. 27:19 BSB). To really get to know someone (his character and who he is), you need to know his heart.

Think about your own experience in relationships. As you get to know someone, you feel like you are *really* getting to know her only when you go beyond the basic, mundane facts about her and get to know her at the level of her desires, purposes, and motives. There is a big difference between statements like "I was born in 1969" or "I am 5 foot 10" and "I struggle with pride and selfishness" or "I am greedy for sexual fulfillment and wrestle with how little my husband pays attention to me" or "I might sound humble, but I wrestle with self-hatred."

To be clear, facts are not useless, and some facts are more useful than others. Knowing that someone was abused is more important than knowing her favorite color. But, at best, facts are just the beginning of a breadcrumb trail we can follow as we seek to draw out the desires, purposes, and motives of the heart.

What Is in the Heart Is Expressed through Our Behavior

In the book of Luke, we find Jesus talking about trees:

> No good tree bears bad fruit, nor again does a bad tree bear good fruit, for each tree is known by its own fruit. For figs are not gathered from thornbushes, nor are grapes picked from a bramble bush. The good person out of the good treasure of his heart produces good, and the evil person out of his evil treasure produces evil, for out of the abundance of the heart his mouth speaks. (6:43–45)

Jesus's primary aim here is not to give a botany lesson but to teach us about how human beings work. The tree represents a person. We can learn a lot about him by looking at him and observing the fruit of his life.

What is the term *fruit* referring to? In this text, it refers to what the good or evil person says. But more generally, fruit is everything that flows from his heart—his words, his thoughts, his actions, his feelings, his plans, and his dreams.

What we learn is *the tree determines the fruit*. Good trees produce good fruit; bad trees produce bad fruit. There is a relationship between the *nature* of the tree and the *quality* of the fruit it produces.

Similarly, *a person's heart determines his life*. Jesus says that a person's life is an outflowing of his heart. What is stored in his heart spills out into his actions. If he's stored up good, good flows out. If he's stored up evil, evil flows out. Have you ever said something and then thought, "I didn't mean that" or "That came out of nowhere"? What you said didn't come out of "nowhere"; it came from your heart!

God's Word Cuts to the Heart

Fortunately, we are not left alone in this journey. God has given us his Word and his Spirit to address matters of the heart. The author of Hebrews writes, "The word of God is living and active, sharper than any two-edged sword, piercing to the division of soul and of spirit, of joints and of marrow, and discerning the thoughts and intentions of the heart" (Heb. 4:12). God's Word is not a dead, old, worn-out book. It's living and active. It's like a sharp double-edged sword. Rightly wielded, it's a powerful instrument. The Word of God cuts deeply into the soul of a porn struggler. It doesn't literally cut between the soul and spirit, joints and marrow. Rather, it pierces and divides him in the most profound, deep, and sensitive ways. Like a scalpel in the hands of a skilled surgeon, it can excise disease and damaged tissue.

The Word also reveals the thoughts and intentions of the heart. There will be times when Scripture, rightly used, unveils hidden areas and motivations in a struggler's heart that lead her into sexual temptation. But it's exactly in these moments, when the struggler is exposed, that the Word also offers hope and freedom.

PRACTICAL IMPLICATIONS

If these principles are true, then our primary aim is to address the struggler's heart, guided by the Word of God. We can do this in two ways.

Address the Root, Not Just the Fruit

Often as we meet with a Christian who is regularly viewing porn or has recently stumbled, we address the fruit of her life:

- When did she look at pornography?
- How long has she been viewing pornography?
- What were her access points?
- What accountability measures does she have in place? Did she use any of the measures?

If we ask questions *only* about the fruit, we lose an opportunity to address the heart-level roots that are creating it. We can get so caught up with talking about a struggler's behaviors and rearranging the circumstances of her life—showing her how to install Internet filter programs, safely use computers or mobile phones, adjust her daily schedule to minimize temptation, guard her eyes, and think carefully about her living situation. While all these things are important, they don't define *why* she does what she does.

If we only address the obvious fruit, our counseling becomes one-dimensional and ignores the roots that feed the behavior. To figure out what motivates a porn struggler, dig out the roots of the tree—the motivations of his heart. Ask heart-oriented questions such as

- Whose approval in your life can make or break your day?
- What does a "good" day look like for you? What about a "bad" day?
- At times when you're tempted to reach out for pornography, what are some of the dominant emotions you're feeling?
- When you're tempted, what promise of God do you tend to forget?
- When you're tempted, what attribute of God do you tend to forget?
- What do you most want, crave, desire, or wish for?
- What do you daydream or fantasize about?
- When you have had a difficult day at work or with others, where or to whom do you turn?

This is a small sampling of questions to get you beyond the superficial. Granted, some strugglers lack self-awareness and don't have a decent grasp of their hearts. Some are just not all that self-reflective. (Most men can easily talk about a basketball game or the latest NFL game but cringe when you start asking intrusive questions.) So be patient as you ask heart-oriented questions. For a few, this will be the first time someone has pressed into their lives. Digging out goals and motivations takes love, gentle persistence, and prayer. Heart work is hard work, but the riches available if you get access to a person's heart are worthy of your efforts.

Pay Attention to Circumstantial, Situational, and Relational Factors That Impact and Influence the Heart

Our hearts do not operate in a vacuum. The hearts of strugglers are influenced by an infinite amount of variables they experience day in and day out. We don't want to "[ignore] the context in which [they] live life" or "[conclude] that the context is *determinative* of the way [they] live life."[2] In other words, a struggler can't blame her porn struggles on her bad day, her angry boss, or her parents' poor job of raising her. Those circumstances and relational factors shape and influence her heart, but they don't make her type in a web address and stare at a screen. Those actions are driven by the ugliness that resides in the caverns of her heart.

As disciplers, we strive to understand a person's world, his relationships, his physical weaknesses and limitations, his past history and family of origin, and many more things about his context. As we seek to correct an imbalance that is created when we ignore heart issues, we don't want to create a similar imbalance by forgetting the larger context for the struggler's life. His circumstances are never the cause of his sin, but they can significantly impact his heart's ability to choose the right path in the midst of temptation.

Reflect: As you counsel your friend, consider the following: Do your questions and conversations probe the heart, or do you go after more superficial information? Do you ask heart-oriented questions ("What makes you tick? Why did you do that? What are you worshipping right now? What do you want out of life? What you do you want from God?"), or do you tend to ask circumstance-oriented questions ("How's your work going? What did you think about the football game last night?")?

Act: Take a risk in your next conversation: ask a more heart-oriented question and pray that the Lord opens up a deeper conversation.

3

DEVELOPING A PLAN

We don't change so we can prove ourselves to God.
We're accepted by God so we can change.
—*Tim Chester,* You Can Change

The simple believes everything,
but the prudent gives thought to his steps.
—*Proverbs 14:15*

As the saying goes, those who fail to prepare, prepare to fail. Parents, mentors, and teachers have conveyed this message countless times. Teenagers hear it and respond, "Yeah, Dad, I know" (possibly with an eye roll too). Unfortunately, many fail to heed this wisdom and find themselves in predicaments that could have been prevented with better preparation.

In our personal experience as counselors, we're astonished that pornography strugglers are so often ill-prepared. What's common is a generic blend of mediocre resolve, haphazard accountability practices, and white-knuckling through hard moments. Given how often believers fall back into sin, this is clearly not enough. Wisdom dictates that we need a strategy—a thoughtful, grace-filled, Christ-centered way out of this problem.

The Bible is all about strategic living, or wisdom. The wise man gives thought to his steps (see Prov. 6:6; 14:15). He follows through on his thoughts and beliefs with actions (see James 1:22). The godly do not lean on their own understanding (see Prov. 3:5) but are hungry for instruction (see Prov. 16:16, 20). They seek counsel from many (see Prov. 15:22), listen carefully to them (see Prov. 12:15), and entrust their plans to the Lord. They know that ultimately his purposes will prevail (see Prov. 19:21).

Wisdom seeks a plan in the face of ongoing sin. It doesn't wander aimlessly. It thinks carefully about how to defeat sin and grow in faith. We are not saying a plan is redemptive or has the power to change someone's heart. It isn't, and it can't. However, a solid, well-thought-out plan can function as a vital tool in this battle.

When people try plans and fail, too often they give up rather than giving their plans a fresh look and retooling them. If they assessed their failed plans, they would likely discover that the failure came from some common problems. Some plans are *incomplete*: a believer attacks one front—confessing to accountability—only to leave another front abandoned; she rarely seeks the Lord in his Word or through prayer. Other plans are *poorly executed*: a guy walks away from his accountability with solid instructions to put filter software on his computer, but he never does it, and no one ever checks on him. Certain plans are *moralistic*: They lack gospel truth, grace, and love. They never point to Jesus; rather, the struggler spends most of her time working at behavior modification. Others are *individualistic*: A sinner fights through his problems on his own. He's convinced that he can defeat the problem and that he doesn't need anyone's help.

THE FOUR INGREDIENTS OF A SOLID BATTLE PLAN

What's a good plan? What's going to help your friend to climb out of the ditch he's created by his chosen slavery? What's going to cover all his bases and not leave any room for the Evil One to wreak havoc? We'll suggest four things.

Your Plan Needs to Be *Comprehensive*

Imagine a general who is plotting out a strategy to defeat his enemy. The general sends his air force—fighter jets, helicopters, bombers, and stealth planes—to go in advance of the ground troops. He organizes the land soldiers to descend on the enemy territory with the full force of their weaponry, tanks, and artillery. But he ignores the seas. He knows his enemy has battleships and submarines, but the general opts to leave out the seas from his strategic plans. How confident would you feel about the general's war plans? Would you want him defending your homeland, especially if you lived just off the coastal waters?

Consider the war against pornography. A lack of a comprehensive plan is a common problem. No war is won by poor planning.

- Mia had monitoring software on her computer yet left her phone unprotected. She knew she should put something on her phone—she just never got around to it.
- Elijah went to church and read his Bible but didn't meet up with accountability. He was slow to build relationships, which meant he was struggling far too frequently on his own.
- Sophia read books on how to defeat porn, but she never prayed about it. She didn't ask for the Lord's help.
- Benjamin was very quick to confess and be transparent about his sin, but he never read his Bible. He leaned on others but didn't go to God with his troubles.
- Clara was self-reflective by nature, so she did the hard work of figuring out her sin patterns and heart issues. However, she didn't know what practical steps to take in fighting her sin.

Why do strugglers and disciplers execute incomplete plans? Why aren't they more thorough? Sometimes it's a matter of *ignorance*—the discipler and sinner know to do some things but not others. For example, Sebastian encouraged Carter to attend church and confess regularly, but he didn't know how to get to deeper heart issues. Other times, it's *laziness* and *apathy*—Patrice knew she had to take active steps to fight her sin, but she just didn't care anymore. At other times, it's a matter of *pride*—Johnny messed up again, but he didn't want to have to confess to his wife, Emery, all over again. Add to this *selfishness, self-justification, self-condemnation,* and *shame,* and there is an abundance of reasons why plans are lacking.

39

To avoid these pitfalls, you must set out to build a more comprehensive plan—one that doesn't let important things slip through the cracks.

Your Plan Needs to Be *Public*[1]

Individual Christianity is an oxymoron. God never meant for believers to fight on their own. The devil loves to isolate Christians. It's a typical part of his strategy—get them to think that they are the only ones in church who are struggling, or that they are the worst of sinners, or that God doesn't care. A struggler fights an internal war against *himself* as well as Satan—his own guilt, shame, lies, and rationalizations of his sin all keep him trapped in a dark corner and far away from the light of Scripture.

For strugglers, going public means coming out of the dark spaces where they tend to hide, like Adam and Eve behind a tree listening to God's approaching footsteps. It means speaking to others, exposing their lives, and being transparent. Humility recognizes the folly of an individualistic mindset. It rushes to be alongside mature believers and begs for help. It's a posture that knows that fighting sin is a serious business and therefore that it requires assistance from those who are deep in wisdom.

The traditional approach to getting help is to find an accountability partner. This is a courageous first step. But biblical living requires more than one teammate. A football game is not won by a quarterback alone. It's won by an entire team. This battle is won by the struggler's entrusting her soul to a community of believers, even if most of them don't personally know about her struggles with sexual sin. It's won by having her not just engage in conversations but also watch living examples of faith, hope, and trust. It's won by drawing her in to be a part of a church.

Your Plan Must Be *Gospel-Driven*

A basic impulse of any human being is for him to rely on himself. Pride makes him want to defeat his problems on his own. He thinks, "I got this. I can take this on." In the face of sexual sin, he comes up with plans that are rooted in his own abilities, finite wisdom, strength, and strategies, but that's all. We guarantee that a strategy of moralistic, self-motivated self-reformation will fail to defeat sexual sin.

For a struggler, the beginning of hope is for him to recognize his need for help outside himself. His plans can't be built around fixing himself but must be driven by faith in a person. His victory is secure not in his plans but in Jesus's work of dying for sinners. Jesus has defeated the penalty and the power of sin and secured victory for sinners. He's already won the war. He's already defeated death and the devil. The stone has been rolled away, and the tomb stands empty. Christ has shown that he will be triumphant.

What's required of strugglers is faith in Jesus—in his saving work on the cross, in his redeeming love for sinners, in his willingness to be obedient unto death. Faith in Christ puts floundering Christians on the trajectory toward success.[2] It's what makes our approach more than just the feeble plan of human minds. Our strategy rises or falls not in a man's attempts to defeat his sin but in his faith in Christ and Christ's victory at Calvary.

Your Plan Must Be *Wise*

Wisdom is our ability to take our knowledge of biblical principles and apply it to the nooks and crannies of daily life. The fool doesn't consider the specifics of her circumstances and how to adjust accordingly. Wisdom descends into the trenches, scouts out its particular surroundings, and figures out practical steps, responses, and forward strategies for living a godly life.

Sadie knew that she couldn't have a personal laptop or phone in her apartment by herself. Living on her own, she was bound to fall to temptation. She was not yet strong enough to resist. Levi could have a phone and computer in his place because he was never alone. He lived in a group home with twelve Christians and was constantly surrounded by others. When Levi viewed his phone or computer, the screen was always visible to those around him. That was the commitment he made to his buddies.

41

Sadie and Levi followed the same principle—they were careful how they handled open access to the Internet. But the principle had different applications—in one case, no technology at home; in another, careful use of devices at home.

WINNING A MULTIFRONT WAR

During World War I, the Germans came up with a strategy known as the Schlieffen Plan to take over Europe and Russia while avoiding a multifront war.[3] Count Alfred von Schlieffen feared he couldn't maintain two fronts, fighting the Allied forces in the west and the Russians in the east. His plan was to focus his forces in the western front, then rush his troops to the eastern front when the time was appropriate. The Kaiser (supposedly) proclaimed, "Paris for lunch; dinner at St. Petersburg."

History shows that the Schlieffen Plan failed. Focusing on one side and neglecting the other lost Germany the war. Success comes as you strategize to buttress and maintain every front of the battle.

Your friend's fight with pornography is the same. There is a war for his soul (see 1 Peter 2:11), and, to win, you must be mindful of every front. Your friend's enemies are not the Allied or Russian forces but the carnal cravings of his heart that run amok, the devil's constant temptations and sexually seductive promises of pleasure, and the world's demands that he mock God and abandon his faith. These enemies—both within and without—oppose his pursuit of holiness and purity.

These enemies will strike anywhere, and the struggler should not focus on one area while overlooking others. You know the trouble with disjointed strategies—fighting on one front and not adequately battling on the other fronts. Jada can't succeed by combating the temptations of movies or videos on her phone but ignoring greedy and selfish tendencies that have erupted in her heart. Derrell can't run to the Lord in guilt, tears, and shame every time he falls and yet be sporadic in his church attendance and Bible reading. Jordan can't live in constant conflict with his spouse and expect himself to hold his own when an attractive woman flirts with him at work. The devil knows that weakness on one front spells doom, so he'll throw his resources where he knows the struggler is weakest.

In the war against sexual sin and pornography, your friend must maintain four fronts as she fights the world, the devil, and her own heart. She must keep an eye on her relationship with *God*, relationship with *self*, relationship with *other people*, and reaction to specific *circumstances*. Every believer's goal is to live with hope, godliness, and purity in all four of these fronts.

The God Front

The most important front is the *God front*. How a person lives in relation to the Lord is the beginning, middle, and end for the entire Christian life. We could just as well call this the *faith front*. Anything regarding a person's spiritual life—sin, trust in Christ, guilt and shame, justification, righteous living, obedience, and so on—makes up this front.

The Circumstance Front

The *circumstance front* takes into account the daily strategies that a struggling believer exercises: maintaining routines, handling technology, and setting up proper boundaries, as well as any other adjustments that are made for his or her specific context. It's on this front that we compose and execute a wise, practical plan for the believer's life.

The People Front

The *people front* consists of the network of relationships, both good and bad, mediocre and glorious, that we all have. Sexual sin hurts these relationships and damages how a struggler views other people; it disrupts healthy relationships; it wreaks havoc with marriages and distorts strugglers' perceptions of genuine, God-glorifying intimacy with fellow believers. It sexualizes what should be pure; it compromises what should be holy and honorable.

The Self Front

The *self front* has two areas—the *embodied self* and the *soul*. The Lord made your friend to be a wonderful combination of body and soul. She must keep tabs on her internal life, governing her thoughts, feelings, and desires. There's an internal war that revolves around her heart and mind. There are battles within her. But she must also consider her body. If she ignores her physical existence, she denies the way God made her and how our Redeemer (in the end) will clothe her with an imperishable and glorious body in eternity. Sexual lusts, especially if engaged over the long haul, rewrite her brain and her neurochemistry. She needs to come to grips with how the gospel changes not just her soul but also her body.

Factoring in all four of these fronts doesn't guarantee victory, but it builds out a better plan for fighting the war. Remember, the victory is assured through Christ's death and resurrection, and as you come up with a plan to help your friend, faith is required on your part and his.

Reflect: Has your approach been haphazard? Measure what you're already doing against the four ingredients of a solid battle plan. To what extent is it comprehensive, public, gospel-driven, and wise?

Act: If the devil is attacking on one of the fronts and weakening your friend, start making plans for how to shore up that battle front. Don't leave any side of her homeland exposed to his merciless attacks.

4

EXECUTING YOUR PLAN: GOD AND CIRCUMSTANCES

*In sex you are either worshiping God by willingly submitting
to his wise and good rules or writing your own rules, and in so
doing, telling yourself that you're smarter than God.*
—*Paul David Tripp,* Sex in a Broken World

Finally, be strong in the Lord and in the strength of his might.
—*Ephesians 6:10*

In the last chapter, we laid out the multifront war against pornography and sexual sin. In this war, our one overarching strategy is to rely on the victory secured through Christ at the cross. Our goal in this chapter and the next is to spell out in greater detail the four fronts of the war: God, circumstances, self, and other people.

As we survey the topography of the battlefield and lay out our strategy for a multifront war, don't be overwhelmed. Eventually, you'll pursue *all* these areas, because if you carelessly ignore exposed and weakened battle fronts, the devil will take advantage of your friend. He's a master tactician, and he's plotting to make sure your friend loses. It will take a good bit of work for you to keep tabs on everything. It's far too easy to focus your energy and time on one side of the war and lose track of the others.

Practically speaking, you won't be able to cover all four fronts in one or two conversations. Gospel relationships are a long-term project. Many of these topics are pursued over the course of months, even years, as you disciple your friend and watch her grow in greater love, knowledge, and discernment.

We'll start with the God and circumstance fronts. What's vital for us to know about both of these?

THE GOD FRONT

The *God front* (or *faith front*) outlines our approach to spiritual issues in the life of the struggler. It details how the believer relates to God in faith or unbelief.

Here are a few ways to strengthen the struggling believer on the God front.

Ask about the Struggler's Personal Relationship with God

Talk to your friend about his personal relationship with God. Who is God, and how does he relate to him? How does he see God—as a loving Father, as cold and distant, as a mean dictator, as a forever-forgiving friend? Does he love God and trust him? Does he feel close to God? Or is he too ashamed to approach him?

How the porn struggler thinks about God affects everything in her life. Theology matters for how we live. Those who have been battling pornography for years commonly believe that *God is good* (a theological truth) *but is not good to them* (personal application of the truth). Because a struggler mistakenly thinks God doesn't help her, she has less godly motivation to fight her sin, and she's more vulnerable to discouragement and shame. Someone who has struggled far too many years and tried everything she knows to do has evidence, in her mind, that amounts to a charge against God that he must not care anymore.

Theology creates a grid through which we see the world. A struggler's distorted view of God undermines her fight against pornography. We need to help a discouraged believer to see who God is—to personally understand the Lord's character and his love. If the porn struggler can't see God rightly, she will ultimately lose this battle.

Ask about Other Sin Struggles

As you help your friend, ask about his typical sin struggles. Not just with sexual sin, but *all* his sin struggles. Not all struggles look alike, so you honor your friend by getting to know his *specific* troubles and his *specific* heart issues in his *specific* circumstances. Figure out what sins he is prone to and how much, and for how long, he has fed his sinful nature.

Consider also the sins that are typical coconspirators with pornography struggles—anger, fear, folly, and pride. Think about the bad fruit that comes from sexual sin. Masturbation commonly plagues sexual strugglers. Porn struggles complicate relationships. Disappointment, fear of man, avoidance—all these things make relationships harder and more frustrating.

Look for True Repentance

Repentance is our sorrow over what we've done wrong (see 2 Cor. 7:10). It turns away from sin, renounces it, and turns back to God (see Prov. 28:13; Ezek. 33:11). Repentance is key to the sinner's survival because it's the first step in a believer's return to God. A Christian can't generate enough self-will to defeat his sin. *God* grants repentance. The Lord quickens his conscience with conviction of sin. As disciplers, we must do the hard work of distinguishing fake repentance from godly sorrow that produces genuine repentance. (We'll look at this in more detail in chapter 9.)

As Christians grow comfortable with their sexual sin, they lose the ferocious edge they need to win this battle. Passivity is gross neglect. No one ignores a tumor. Porn, a cancerous problem, grows if we leave it alone. For the Christian empowered by the Holy Spirit and the Word, only an aggressive disposition against sexual sin is acceptable.

Build Up Faith in Christ

You should ask about the shape and contours of a struggler's faith in Christ. Is she fighting for faith, or has she given up? Faith in Christ is the chief goal of Christian discipleship. Without the shield of faith (see Eph. 6:16), Christian warriors will not be able to guard against the fiery darts of the Evil One.

A struggler can feel hopeless. But, in Christ, she can find hope again. As you call her to put her faith in Christ and not in her ability to fix things, to find forgiveness by Christ's blood and not in some miraculous turnaround, to find comfort fundamentally in the shadow of the cross and not in some magical formula, her hope slowly returns. It starts to spill over into her life and wash away her despair. Her faith grows stronger.

Loving a believer means helping her to ground her life in Christ. She needs to taste and see that the Lord is good and that the Lord will deliver her (see Ps. 34). She needs to know the gospel and experience its sweetness as a balm for her soul (see Isa. 53; Mark 10:43–45; 2 Cor. 5:21). She needs to embrace her union with Christ (see Rom. 6:1–7:6).

Ground the Struggler in the Gospel through Spiritual Disciplines

I (Deepak) grew up watching my father marinate chicken or fish in a rich batter to give it more flavor. For the porn addict, marinating means being in sustained contact with gospel realities. A porn struggler needs to soak daily in gospel truths. *Sustained gospel contact is essential for his survival.*

Being in church, studying the Word, sitting under good preaching, praying, enjoying rich Christian fellowship, and seeking out wise, godly counsel are not optional for the believer, nor are they add-ons to discipling or counseling. Spiritual disciplines and the common means of grace can't be neglected. Often they are the means that God uses to rescue a person's soul from the pit of hell. They are life-sustaining means of pursuing a wholehearted relationship with Christ. The Word brings life. Prayer and regular communion with God keep faith vibrant. If we see friends spending less time in the Word, less time in prayer, and less time face-to-face with others (see Ps. 119:9–10), we should grow concerned.

Ask what your friend's time in God's Word looks like. We guarantee that there is a one-to-one correlation between her ability to flee temptation and her time in the Word. We've had porn addicts say,

"This week I was consistent in my devotional time. I've had a rich time soaking up the Word. And guess what? I didn't watch pornography or masturbate." To them, it's a shocking development. To us, not so much. Is it outside the realm of possibility for someone to be in God's Word and still view pornography? No. But in our experience it's unusual for the two to be able to peacefully coexist.

This means that teaching porn strugglers how to dig deeply into the Word is a vital means of discipleship. What good is it to talk often about sexual sin when they don't know how to find daily nourishment for their souls? Spiritual hunger and dryness lead to death in this fight. Too often, those who struggle with pornography dismiss the redemptive power that comes from reading God's Word. The Bible attests to its own power: "How can a young man keep his way pure? By guarding it according to your word" (Ps. 119:9).

The spiritual discipline of fasting is an unexpected ally in this fight, but it shouldn't be. In fasting, people withhold physical delights so as to narrow their focus to spiritual matters, and it has the additional benefit of curbing their carnal desires. More porn strugglers should try fasting!

Of course, if we hand a Christian a spiritual to-do list and put pressure on him to perform, he will fail, and we shouldn't be surprised if he continues to cycle in and out of his addiction. A genuine love for Christ must be at the root of everything he does, with obedience as the fruit of his affection for his Savior. Change starts not with the believer but with God, who gives him the strength in his inner being to fight this battle (see Eph. 3:16).

Listen to a Struggler's Spiritual Concerns

Some believers are overrun with pornography and discouraged by the battle, finding themselves losing more often than winning. Consequently, they wonder if they are Christians. "How can a true believer keep sinning like this? I say I trust Christ, but I keep looking at this filth. What's wrong with me?" Struggles with assurance linger under the surface, so you should ask about them. Christ isn't intimidated by a struggler's hard questions, so you shouldn't be either.

49

THE CIRCUMSTANCE FRONT

The *circumstance front* highlights the daily situations believers find themselves in. Fighting on this front involves monitoring strugglers' use of technology, their access to pornography, their daily schedules, their ability to fight temptation, and much more.

Although the God front is the most *important* in this war, the circumstance front is the most *urgent*. Think in terms of medical triage. What if you walked into an emergency room profusely bleeding, and the charge nurse said, "Sit down, and we'll be with you in thirty minutes"? You'd be angry, right? Can't she see that you're dying? When medical triage is done correctly, the most urgent matters are treated first. If a patient has a life-threatening wound, a doctor or nurse tends to it before he or she does anything else.

The same thing applies to folks struggling with porn. When we first become aware that someone is struggling, we seek to stop the bleeding by addressing the struggler's circumstances. As long as a Christian's mind and heart are overwhelmed with pornography, it's hard to make much progress, especially at a deeper heart level. We'll encourage our friend to be brutal in cutting off open access, and we'll push back on any self-righteous attitude that resists taking this step.

Here are a few ways to strengthen a struggling believer in the circumstance front.

Set Up Boundaries

We construct boundaries to build a firewall around a struggler's heart and mind. These are barriers to inhibit his use of porn, and they may involve software monitoring programs (such as Covenant Eyes), website blockers, and daily strategies (such as turning away from tempting images on a billboard, a computer screen, or a magazine at the supermarket checkout aisle). Think in terms of walls—the thicker the wall that stands between the addict and the pornography, the better chance he has of repelling the carnal desires that motivate his addiction.

Any Christian who trusts in his own abilities to fight porn is a fool. The Scriptures say he's infected with pride. His self-confident belief that he can control the problem keeps him from making the wise choice to put filters on all his devices and build thick barriers in the middle of the struggle. What he needs instead is "sober judgment" (Rom. 12:3)—a realistic, humble perspective on himself, his weaknesses, and his vulnerability to sin. It is far too easy for us to underestimate the power that sin has over our hearts and minds.

While computers used to be the major problem for porn strugglers, now the front line is tablets and smartphones or almost any e-device. What kind of boundaries has the struggler constructed on his smartphone or tablet or laptop? If he is doing nothing, you need to know.

Suppose your friend slips up by watching videos on YouTube that cause him to lust. Because he failed when he faced temptation, he has shown himself to not be responsible enough to handle open and unhindered access to the Internet. To protect himself from his unruly desires, he should cut YouTube out of his life and severely restrict his access to the Internet. He should construct boundary walls to protect himself from his own folly and lack of self-control. He should willingly give up his freedom and access for a season, removing the YouTube app (and any Internet-accessible apps) from all his mobile devices and setting up limits for the hours he can be online. If he resists these steps, claiming they are too radical, then he's not yet ready to put up a decent fight. No soldier goes into a war with an apathetic attitude.

A porn addict may complain, "What's the use? I can find a lot of workarounds. Eventually I'll find my way onto another video platform." The flesh is very creative, we get that. However, that's no excuse for doing nothing. We construct barriers to slow the struggling believer down from committing sin. We make it inconvenient for this believer to sin. He still wants to, and so he does, but we've made his pursuit of sin harder. Even when he's more determined to do it than he was before, we do everything we can to slow him down. That's better for his soul's sake. This is a spiritual war. We'll do whatever is needed in order to preserve his holiness and win this fight.

In our counseling, we convince believers to subscribe to Covenant Eyes (CE) or some form of accountability software. Every week, the software generates a report about the believer's Internet activity and sends it directly to her accountability partner. We ask who will be her accountability and receive the CE reports.

Many men and women don't use monitoring software to fight their temptations. Don't be surprised! Ask your friend to use a monitored browser, remove apps with embedded browsers, close the applications store, and make use of the restrictions function on her phone. Your goal is to build a fortified wall around her lustful heart, so that once you've slowed down the bleeding, heart work can be done.

Examine the Struggler's Temptations

A struggling believer lives in a polluted environment—a society infatuated with sex that offers alluring images at every turn. That makes daily fights against temptation a normal part of the Christian's existence. If we don't take active steps to fend off temptation, we'll end up stuck in a defensive posture as we fight the sin rather than probing the deeper issues that motivate the struggler to sin.

Thus you need to examine the nature of the temptations the struggler typically runs into—what are the normal pressures he faces? What's tantalizing to him? What grabs his attention? What is asking him to turn from God and to indulge in sin? Does he have a sense of how to face these temptations? We'll look at temptations more in chapter 15.

Reduce Danger Zones

As you fight in the circumstance front, pinpoint danger zones and cut them out. The term *danger zones* refers to the times, places, and situations in which a Christian typically struggles. For many single men and women, failure comes whenever they are alone—often late at night, behind closed doors. We can employ strategies to prevent them from stumbling in these danger zones. For example, we may ask a believer to give her laptop to her roommate every night at the same time. She shouldn't be on her laptop in her room without the door wide open and the screen facing the doorway, and she should use her laptop, tablet, or smartphone in a common area whenever possible.

We cover how to talk about heart issues in chapter 2, "Targeting the Heart." We show how to sort through the coconspirators with our lusts in chapter 11, "Taking a Wider Gaze at Sin."

A smart battle plan highlights the situations and contexts where sin is often provoked; it is conscious of how to make proper adjustments. A believer who has had an overwhelming day in a toxic work environment plans for stress relief when she gets home that night. She plans to hide behind a closed door to escape the unrealistic pressures of her day. We make changes in her circumstances because these can slow her down from sinning.

However, as helpful as it is to cut out danger zones, doing so doesn't ultimately solve the war in a struggler's heart. That's what we'll look at in the next chapter.

Reflect: If you've begun helping your friend, where in the God and circumstance fronts has your discipling fallen short? What adjustments do you need to make in your plan? If you're not yet discipling your friend, how can you begin? Use the checklist below to help you to pinpoint places where you should retool your current plan.

THE GOD FRONT

- Help him to grow in his personal relationship with the Lord.
- Explore sexual sin's coconspirators (such as anger, fear, pride, foolishness) and bad fruit.
- Distinguish between genuine and fake repentance.
- Encourage faith in Christ and a strong affection for him.
- Fortify spiritual disciplines and other means of grace—time in the Word, prayer, and even fasting!
- Ask him about his struggles with assurance.

THE CIRCUMSTANCE FRONT

- Cut out access to pornography by locking down the believer's electronic devices. Deal with all of them.
  - o Secure filter programs.
  - o Get rid of the app store.
  - o Employ restrictions.
  - o Use monitored browsers.
  - o Give a discipler or roommate the administrative password for her restrictions.
- Understand the nature of the believer's specific temptations and how to fight them.
- Cut out the danger zones and situations where sexual sin is provoked.

Act: When we ask about spiritual disciplines, most people default to Bible reading and prayer. Most don't consider fasting at all in their race toward godliness and faithfulness. Perhaps that is due to the fact that fasting is normally related to food—fasting from eating. How about asking your friend to fast from technology? Yes, there may be times when he needs a laptop or phone for work, but there is a great deal of technology and media that he can abstain from: radio, talk radio, cable TV, movie and television streaming services, movies, music streaming services and podcasts, and so on. Here's the challenge for your friend: Can he spend a week cutting out all excess noise so that he can revitalize and renew his relationship with God? Notice the purpose for fasting—it's not to draw attention to his own ascetic abilities (see Col. 2:23) but to deepen his relationship with God (see Joel 2:12).

5

EXECUTING YOUR PLAN:
SELF AND OTHER PEOPLE

*If you are caught in a sin, you need to be
restored by someone who lives by the Spirit.*
—Heath Lambert, Finally Free

*For the grace of God has appeared, bringing salvation for all people,
training us to renounce ungodliness and worldly passions, and to live
self-controlled, upright, and godly lives in the present age.*
—Titus 2:11–12

In the last two chapters, we described the four fronts of the war we
are fighting against pornography. Any such war will be lost if we
don't keep tabs on all four fronts to protect our friends from the
devil's tactics.

We've seen that the *God front* refers to a struggler's relationship
with the Lord in faith and unbelief and covers the different parts
of his spiritual life, such as repentance, sin, guilt, justification, and
shame. On the *circumstance front*, we maintain daily practical strategies to help our struggling friends to face temptation in their specific
life contexts. We cut off access to the Internet; build boundaries,
daily routines, and habits; and strategize about how to face common
temptations.

We don't want to leave ourselves vulnerable on the battlefield, so
we need to cover two more fronts: the *self front* and the *people front*.
You will complete your battle plan by considering how your friend's

heart, mind, and body need to be addressed and how his relationships need to fortify him in his ongoing battle against lust.

THE SELF FRONT

The self front highlights both your friend's embodied and his internal self. The term *embodied* describes your friend's physical, bodily existence. The word *internal* indicates his thoughts, feelings, desires, and intentions.

The *Embodied* Self

The physical part of the self is vital because God the Creator made men and women to be physical beings. In Genesis 1, he deemed their physical existence good. He made them with the ability to eat, drink, smell, sleep, touch, feel, and have sex. He made an intricate system of brain, organs, muscles, nerves, flesh, and blood, all of which remarkably come together to form a living, breathing, thinking, talking human being.

A porn struggle starts out when a sinner voluntarily makes foolish choices. If she continues to choose sexual sin, the underlying neurochemistry of her brain and body changes. (We'll look at this more in chapter 19, "Understanding and Disciplining the Body.") You will need to acknowledge this reality and adjust accordingly for it. Don't reduce a person to mere neurons, but also don't ignore the ways that her body changes because of her ongoing, addictive sexual sin.

A proper diet, exercise, and sleep are foundational building blocks for anyone's life. Curtail or mess with these building blocks, and your friend's struggle against sexual sin will be harder. So keep tabs on her sleep patterns. How often people waste time thumbing mindlessly through random photos and posts when they could be sleeping! A good night's sleep establishes rhythms of work and rest. Tiredness weakens a struggler's defenses and makes her more vulnerable in the daily battle against sin and Satan. Sleep recharges and refreshes her. Do you underestimate the value of rest in the fight against sexual sin?

Also watch the struggler's exercise and diet. A believer's lack of self-control doesn't just impact how he uses technology but may also lead him to overeat and not exercise. Glorifying God with his body involves every aspect of his existence: eating, drinking, exercising, and sleeping!

The *Internal* Self

Remember, our overarching war strategy involves fortifying the circumstance front. Once we have good filters and barriers in place, we've made it extremely difficult for a struggler to access porn. We then see a shift from his *external* battles (such as temptations to look lustfully at scantily clad women on a screen) to his *internal* world (his heart, mind, thoughts, and emotions). The sinful flesh is not going to give up this fight easily. The internal war—the war for a struggler's heart and mind—is where the battle is usually won or lost.

Through your work to adjust her circumstances and build solid boundary walls, your friend can get to a place where she is doing well in fighting off external temptations. Just because she is finding success in fighting external temptations doesn't mean she's mastered internal self-control, however. Solomon advised his son, "A man without self-control is like a city broken into and left without walls" (Prov. 25:28). Walls were used to keep city dwellers safe, so the people in a city that no longer has walls lack protection from their enemies. Similarly, lack of self-control puts a man or woman in a perilous place without strong protection from internal temptations (sinful desires and lusts that rule the heart) and external temptations (the devil's attacks using porn websites, worldly messages, and so on). Living in a vulnerable position, without any boundaries to protect against bandits, is sure way for a person to get himself killed. Thus, the struggler's war requires additional tactics to protect the internal self.

Build up an identity that is rooted in the gospel. Out of our sense of self, we form our identities. Many strugglers live with identities that are defined more by failure than by a genuine relationship with Christ. A struggler's sense of personal failure and his self-condemnation can be so strong that his identity is overwhelmingly defined by what he *does* (looks at porn) rather than who he *is* (a child of God). Rather than thinking, "I'm a Christian who struggles with porn," most days he thinks, "I'm a porn addict." His thoughts about himself are godless at their core.

The greater a believer's sense of love, acceptance, and forgiveness in Christ, the more strength she will have to fight her battles. We fan the flames of faith in Christ because we want to see the struggler root her identity in the gospel. We ground our conversations in the Word, pray regularly for the Lord's help, and consistently point to Christ as our hope. What she ultimately does in the fight against porn flows out of her relationship with Christ. Imperatives (what she *does* to please God) flow out of the indicatives (who she *is* in Christ).

Engage and encourage the struggler's heart. As we saw in chapter 2, the term *heart* in the Bible describes the core or central part of who we are. Some have called the heart our command center, for in our hearts reside the desires, motivations, hopes, dreams, sins, and attitudes that shape our lives (see Matt. 12:33–35; Luke 6:43–45; James 3:14). Out of our hearts come the thoughts, feelings, and actions that overflow from our hearts' desires and attitudes. Helping a struggler means engaging and encouraging his heart.

Kill and replace bad desires. As we'll see in more detail in chapter 16, a believer who is enslaved to pornography is held captive by his desires. He looks at explicit images, feeding the desires of the sinful flesh, and those desires grow stronger and motivate him to choose sin again and again. It's a chosen slavery. His selfish desire for porn grows, and grows, and grows, and eventually overtakes his life. As a discipler, you'll encourage your struggling friend to starve the bad inordinate desires, with the goal of killing them off completely, and to replace carnal desires with good desires rightly ordered by God's Word. A believer's chief spiritual desire should be a greater affection for Christ.

Engage the lies or self-justifications that allow a believer to downplay the problem and stay stuck in his sin. A struggler talks to himself about the problem, saying, "It's not that big a deal" or "I can get control of it" or "It's not going to hurt anyone" or "When I'm married, this will all go away" or even "I don't want to burden other people." Through this internal dialogue, he is preaching a false gospel to himself—candy-coated lies that allow him to coddle his sin rather than let it go. Draw these thoughts out, expose them to the light, and encourage the struggler to reject them.

Don't overlook the struggler's guilt and shame. Guilt and shame are different, as we'll see in more detail in chapter 18, and they require different responses.

Guilt describes a struggler's state of culpability and condemnation before God for her sin. Due to the repetitive nature of this problem, guilt piles on top of guilt, creating a large trash pile in her soul. We're not surprised when a struggler uses vivid language, such as saying she feels like "a dog return[ing] to its vomit" (Prov. 26:11 NIV). Press into the guilt and encourage true repentance.

Shame is a Christian's embarrassment before God and others. Scripture gives us descriptions of shame that help us to know what to do with it, and we talk about these descriptions in more detail in chapter 18. In short, we assist the struggler by thinking through with her these biblical ways to describe shame—a sense of being naked and exposed (see Gen. 3:7), unclean and defiled (see Isa. 64:6), outcast and rejected (see Gen. 16), or a failure (see Matt. 26:75). Shame pours forth self-condemnation that overruns her heart and mind. Shame makes a believer hide. Encourage your friend not to run away but to face his shame and expose it, telling the parts of his story that are entangled by shame.

Ask the struggler about his fantasy life. Memories store up over years of viewing. A typical porn user has hundreds of images stored on the hard drive of his brain. It doesn't take much for him to access these images and play an X-rated movie reel in his mind.

Accountability that focuses on behavior only but doesn't engage the mind and heart is insufficient. Admittedly, most believers we counsel are surprised when we ask about their fantasy lives. We never ask in order to learn the grimy details of these addicts' sins. We don't want to know, because it's a stumbling block for our own hearts. Rather, our goal is to know what's going on in order to teach them "to say 'No' to ungodliness" (Titus 2:12 NIV), especially when they are tempted to dwell on images in their minds or make erotic movie reels in their imaginations. By saying no, they are constructing internal boundaries in their minds and hearts.

But just saying no to sinful fantasies is not enough. Unless we fill up the void with righteous thinking and a love for Christ, the flesh will quickly fill it up with other ungodly thoughts and desires. So be very deliberate in encouraging the believer to focus his mind on more godly things (see 2 Cor. 10:4–6; Phil. 4:8).

THE PEOPLE FRONT

Because sexual sin ruins relationships and fosters loneliness, we fight on this fourth front by drawing believers in. We position mature Christians within striking distance of believers who need help to persevere. Our goal is vulnerability and transparency with members of a close circle of friends and mentors. Like mold, sin flourishes in the darkness. When a believer brings things to the light, God can transform her sin, and the mold will die.

The responsibility is ultimately on the struggling Christian to build honest, vulnerable, and loving relationships as a means to fight her sexual sin. Do not accept any excuses or rationalizations when it comes to accountability. Here are a few common ones:

- "I don't know anyone at my church well enough to share this."
- "I don't want to burden anyone with my problems."
- "They probably already have enough going on in their own lives."
- "I've tried reaching out for help before, and people never follow through!"

- "I had an accountability partner once, and they had more issues than I did!"

There could be validity to these concerns, based on a struggler's bad experiences in the past. But just because bad accountability exists doesn't mean a struggling believer should ditch accountability altogether. Her goal should be to find the right kind of accountability, which we'll look at in more depth in chapter 7.

It is not unusual for a mentor to have to push a believer beyond his comfort zone to be more vulnerable with other Christians. Sin must be fought in the context of a supernatural community, where we share the burdens of our fellow believers. The struggling Christian doesn't have to tell *everyone*, but he needs to tell a few people. We link arms and journey together to heaven, leaving no soul behind.

Here are a few questions to ask:

- Are her accountability conversations superficial, or are they vulnerable and honest?
- Does he have local accountability partners whom he sees regularly?
- Is she receiving accountability that is rules-based and law-driven, or is it merciful, gracious, and loving?
- Do the mentors who receive his Covenant Eyes reports call him when they see something concerning?

Accountability must be placed in a larger framework of Christian friendship. It is just one part of a larger strategy to disciple a believer into greater faith and maturity in Christ. The struggling believer needs a friend or two to help with sin struggles, but she also needs to grow her faith, build more vulnerable relationships, and learn to apply the gospel to the different aspects of her life.

For this reason, accountability is done in a local church, where the struggling believer is joined to a group of believers in the same community. Church membership is a formal, self-conscious commitment to a local congregation. Membership is a necessary component of Christian faith. Experiencing rich, deep fellowship with believers, sitting under the public preaching of God's Word, participating in the Lord's Supper and baptism, growing relationally and emotionally in connection with an entire community, finding ways to serve— these are all essential ingredients to growing up as a Christian. All this comes not from one accountability relationship but through a connection to an entire church community. The church is indispensable to any plan that hopes to bear the fruit of holiness.

Reflect: If you've begun helping your friend, where on the self and people fronts has your discipling fallen short? What adjustments do you need to make in your plan? If you're not yet discipling your friend, how can you begin? Use the checklist below to help you to pinpoint places where you should retool your current plan.

THE SELF FRONT

The *Embodied* Self
- Encourage good sleep, eating habits, and exercise.
- Help him to grow in self-control and the self-discipline of his body (see 1 Cor. 9:27).

The *Internal* Self
- Encourage a Christ-centered, gospel-grounded identity.
- Engage and encourage her heart.
- Starve inordinate desires and replace the bad desires with a greater affection for Christ.
- Don't let him give in to lies, self-justification, or self-condemnation.
- Help her to overcome guilt and shame.
- Help him to construct internal boundaries in his mind and heart.

- Ask about her fantasy life and her internal battles.
- With the Holy Spirit's help, work to revive his dead conscience.

THE PEOPLE FRONT

- Draw other believers in.
- Don't limit accountability to just one person.
- Work at honest, frequent, local, and tough conversations.
- Don't limit conversations to sexual sin but encourage faith and maturity in Christ.
- Help her to join with a local body of believers and enjoy the fruit of participating in a church community.

Act: If there are places where the self and people fronts are weak, buttress them by talking through them and praying about them with your friend. Ask the Lord for help.

6

ASKING THE RIGHT QUESTIONS

With more questions comes less empathy.
It feels more like an interrogation than a conversation.
—Edward T. Welch, "Questions about Questions"

"Simon, son of John, do you love me more than these?"
[Peter] said to him, "Yes, Lord; you know that I love you."
—John 21:15

In order to help those struggling with pornography, you need to know what sorts of questions to ask. We know that we should ask questions, but oftentimes we are not asking the *right* questions. Take, for example, Eli in 1 Samuel 1:

> As [Hannah] continued praying before the LORD, Eli observed her mouth. Hannah was speaking in her heart; only her lips moved, and her voice was not heard. Therefore Eli took her to be a drunken woman. And Eli said to her, "How long will you go on being drunk? Put your wine away from you." But Hannah answered, "No, my lord, I am a woman troubled in spirit. I have drunk neither wine nor strong drink, but I have been pouring out my soul before the LORD. Do not regard your servant as a worthless woman, for all along I have been speaking out of my great anxiety and vexation." (vv. 12–16)

Eli asked a question ("How long will you go on being drunk?"), but it was not the *right* question because he assumed information based on the circumstances. Eli's poor assumption led him to ask a bad question.

There is a real danger that right now, even as you read this, you are making dozens of assumptions in your relationships. We *all* unhelpfully make assumptions. No exceptions. Unfortunately, when we make assumptions, we fill in information that may or may not be valid. That creates misunderstandings and frustrations, and it blunts our ability to be effective in ministry.

Let's say Torrance has wrestled with pornography over the last few months, but you assume he's struggled with it for years. You talk to him about the effects of porn on a person's mind and body when the struggle is ingrained and has become a long-term battle. Or maybe you are talking with Tina. Before she came to see you, she installed software filters on all her devices. Yet you ask her questions about her Internet access and talk about her need for a stronger firewall, assuming she's got to shut down her access points. In both situations, your assuming disposition communicates "I'm not considerate enough to get to know you well *before* I speak up." This hurts Torrance's and Tina's ability trust you. So the general rule of thumb is never to assume but to ask instead. Ask questions to test the validity or illegitimacy of your assumptions.[1]

To debunk our assumptions, not only do we ask questions, but we try to ask the *right* questions.

ASKING THE RIGHT QUESTIONS

It's easy to ask basic questions that uncover the *circumstances* of a struggler's life: *Who? What? Where? When? How? For how long?* Each of these kinds of questions draws out information that is useful for helping us to understand the person who sits in front of us and his current plight. It's not magical. There is no special formula or secret sauce for asking questions. Many come with common sense, and with experience you grow in knowing what to ask. *What is the problem? When did it happen? How often did you act out? What devices did you use? Where did you do it? What time of day?*

But you'll also get beyond the circumstances and dig a level deeper into a struggler's *inner life*—her thoughts, feelings, and heart issues. Think of this as excavation work. To get to the heart, we've got to plunge one hundred feet below the surface-level, circumstantial issues and ask questions with depth. Depth questions are heart-oriented questions. They go after the goals, motivations, and desires that sit below the surface and define a person's heart. *What motivated you to act? Why did you act out? Were you lonely? Scared? Angry at God? Were you trying to escape stress? What are you worshipping right now? What really matters to you? What makes you tick? What does your life revolve around?* These are the kinds of questions that get the porn struggler to share deeper issues.

You'll explore his *spiritual life*. In fighting the sin, we can get so caught up in the practical and tactical elements (such as blocking access and setting up accountability) that we neglect the struggler's spiritual war. *Does he trust God? Does he believe God can change him? Has he repented, or does he just feel bad for what he did? What does faith look like to him? Does he understand the gospel? Does gospel truth feel cold or hollow, or does it bring him life?*

You'll ask about her *relationships*. Accountability is vital for survival. *Who does she meet with? Who knows about her problem? How connected is she at church? Is the accountability helpful or not so much?* We want to know if she trusts her accountability, if she has oriented her life around a gospel-preaching church, and if she has relationships that breathe hope and life into her. *What relationships bring her joy?*

When asking these targeted questions, your goal is not to accumulate a long list of details or to take the struggler down rabbit trails but rather to lovingly understand the struggler who needs your help.[2] Too often, we offer shortsighted remedies and quick fixes for the addict without doing the due diligence of getting to know the whole person and the good and bad of his world.

Doing this well involves the exegesis of both Scripture and the struggler. If you emphasize understanding Scripture over understanding the person, you could find yourself using Scripture in a way that it was never intended for. If you emphasize understanding the porn struggler over understanding Scripture, you could end up using pragmatic tools and tricks rather than the living Word of God. Understanding *both* Scripture and the porn struggler is indispensable in one-another ministry.

EXAMPLES OF QUESTIONS TO ASK A PORN STRUGGLER

To equip you for the ministry of asking the right questions, we've listed questions below that we have used. These questions are not meant to be repeated verbatim but rather meant to be put into your own natural wording. Ultimately, they are best embedded into a wider conversation. Remember, you are not an FBI interrogator hammering out questions. You are a loving member of the body of Christ who is seeking to speak truth in love.

Origins of the Struggle; Childhood and Family Experiences
- Do you remember when you were first exposed to pornography?
- Do you remember what you felt when you first saw porn?
- Did your parents give you any sort of teaching on sexuality— biblical or otherwise?
- Do you remember talking to your friends about sex?
- How would you describe your general attitude toward sex as you were growing up?
- What was the main message about sex that you took home from your church or community of faith?
- Is there anything else you think I should know about your family background or your childhood?

Circumstances and Context
- Describe the general context you find yourself in when you give in to pornography.
- Are there similar patterns, triggers, times of day, locations, sites, or rituals associated with your pornography use?
- How frequently have you looked at pornography over the last month? Two months? Six months? Year?

- In more general terms, can you give me a history of your sexual immorality? What are your other areas of sexual temptation or struggle?
- Are you watching a specific type or genre of porn?
- How do you fight temptations? Do you cut temptations off early on, when you first experience them as thoughts, feelings, or bodily urges?
- Do you find yourself giving in to temptation when you feel stress? Anger? Loneliness? Isolation? Rejection? Guilt? Boredom? Anxiety? Depression?
- What are your access points to porn? Have you cut off all these access points? Are there *any* vulnerable points that you could break through to access porn in a weak moment? If so, how do we get rid of these vulnerabilities in your firewall?
- What's your overall firewall? What filter programs, blocked websites, and restrictions on your technological devices do you have in place?
- Are *all* the devices secure? Do you have potential access to any old or retired devices?
- Do you have any accountability measures in place?
- What role does your body play in all this? How much do your sense of arousal and bodily urges influence you or drive you?
- How long has the struggle been going on?
- When have you experienced periods of victory?
- Have you noticed your usage and consumption of pornography escalate over time?
- Are you masturbating? Is it tied to your porn use?
- Is there anything else you think I should know about your context that could help me to better understand you as a person?

Inner Life / Internal World

General Overview
- Are you aware of any internal battles in the lead-up to the temptations you experience?

- How much has your sexual sin come to define your sense of identity? Do you see yourself as an addict and a slave to sexual sin or as a child of the living God?
- Do you recognize the Spirit's work in your life? Does he bring you conviction and comfort?
- Do you sense an internal struggle between the Spirit and your flesh?
- How long does this struggle tend to last?
- What tends to help you to win that battle for holiness?
- What tends to push you toward temptation?
- Give me your best metaphor for your internal struggle.
- What role does fantasizing play in your engagement with pornography? When do you indulge your fantasies? What else should I know about your fantasizing?
- Is there anything else that is going on internally that you think it would be helpful for me to know?

Motivation and Causation
- What lies, deficient understandings, self-justifications, and rationalizations keep you sinning?
- Give me your best reason or guess as to why you keep viewing pornography. Escape? Anger at God or yourself? Boredom and loneliness? Self-hatred? A need for affirmation? A desire to numb your emotions after a fight? Control? A sense of entitlement? Discontent with your current life? Maybe some other reason?
- What do you love the most?
- What do you get from your sin?
- Where do you spend the majority of your time, energy, and resources?
- If you could eliminate one factor from your life to help you to make progress in this battle, what would it be, and why?
- If you could add one factor to your life to help you to make progress in this battle, what would it be, and why?
- Do you feel defeated? Have you given up believing that God

can change you? Are you willing to fight, or have you become spiritually apathetic about your sexual sin?

- Is there such thing as a porn-free life? Or does it not exist in your mind?
- Do you have affections and desires for Christ? Is there any longing left in you for him?

God, Faith, Repentance, and Spiritual Life

- When you think of God, what comes to mind? How do you see and understand him? Who was God to you before your struggle? Who is he to you right now?
- What do you think about God in the midst of your struggle? Do you believe God is holy, merciful, loving, compassionate, generous, good, and sovereign?
- Do you think God is powerful enough to change you? If not, why not? In what sense have you given up on God?
- What words of Scripture, hymns of faith, and creedal beliefs do you call to mind in times of temptation?
- What does repentance look like in your life?
- Do you believe you have repented from this sin? If so, why?
- What exactly are you repenting from?
- Are you grieved by your sin? Do you just feel bad because you were caught? Do you feel the weight of having offended God?
- What is the gospel? Have you committed your life wholeheartedly to gospel truth and gospel living? Or do you intellectually acknowledge the gospel but not really believe it or live by it?
- What does your faith look like? Do you fight for belief, or are you struggling with it?
- Do you feel assured that you are a child of God? If not, why not?

Relationships and Accountability

- What would it take for you to open up to others?
- Who knows that you are struggling? What do they know?

- If you don't have accountability, who should you establish it with?
- Do you regularly confess to anyone? A friend? Spouse? Pastor? Accountability partner?
- Is there anyone in your own local church who knows? If not, why not?
- How often do you communicate with your accountability person?
- What does your accountability ask you when you meet up?
- Is there anything they should ask that they don't already ask?
- Are they helpful to you, or is the relationship not really benefiting you?
- What makes for good accountability?
- Is your accountability available to you when you need them? Do you ever feel like a burden to them?
- Who gets your accountability / Covenant Eyes reports? Do they call after they see something wrong on the reports? If they don't call, do you need to ask them to change their practice?
- If the accountability is not working, do you need to find someone else?

Postmortem
- What happens in the aftermath of your viewing pornography?
- Do you have a plan for what to do after a fall? If so, what is it? If not, can we come up with a plan?
- Do you engage in any cycles of guilt, shame, and confession? If so, please describe.
- Do you make promises to yourself, to God, and to others regarding not falling into this temptation again?

As you ask questions, use the helpful phrases and segues below to further the conversation:

- Thank you for sharing that.
- That is really helpful to know.

- Could you elaborate more on that?
- Please, tell me more.
- I've never heard that before. Thank you.
- I can tell this is hard for you to talk about.
- Am I understanding correctly that when you said _____, you meant _____?
- Do you mind if I summarize what I heard you say?

Asking questions is an important part of our role as disciplers. Asking the *right* questions requires wisdom and dependence on the Spirit. May God give us the grace and insight to be instruments in his hands.

Reflect: Go through the questions above and highlight the ones you've never asked before or that you think would be particularly helpful. Don't bombard your struggling friend with them the next time you meet up. Instead, sprinkle a few of these questions into your next few conversations together. Remember, questions operate best when they are embedded in a loving and compassionate conversation, not fired off as though you are a drill sergeant interrogating his subordinates.

Act: Don't be limited by these questions. Rather, use them as a launching pad for deeper, more probing, and richer conversations. By the grace of God, through the conviction of the Spirit, pray that the Lord will let you ask questions that will uncover what needs to be exposed.

7

BECOMING ACCOUNTABILITY THAT WORKS

The next best thing to being wise oneself
is to live in a circle of those who are.
—*C. S. Lewis, "Hamlet: The Prince or the Poem?"*

Bear one another's burdens, and so fulfill the law of Christ.
—*Galatians 6:2*

Do you know what wisdom is? It's not just *knowing* about God and his Word but faithfully *applying* God's Word to everyday life.

Solomon tells us, "Wisdom is the focus of the discerning, but the eyes of a fool wander to the ends of the earth" (Prov. 17:24 BSB). The discerning care so much about wisdom that they make it their focus. Wisdom is better than gold or fine jewels (see Prov. 8:11; 16:16). It's valuable and worth pursuing. Contrast the discerning with the fool, whose eyes roam to the ends of the earth. The fool has no purpose, no focus, and no goals. He wanders through life without clear direction or wisdom to guide him.

King Solomon also writes, "Whoever walks with the wise becomes wise, but the companion of fools will suffer harm" (Prov. 13:20). He warns us, "Take heed to the company you keep." If a struggler walks with wise people, she will become wise. If she chooses to spend time with fools, their foolishness will hurt her—or, even worse, she too will become a fool.

Porn strugglers desperately need wisdom, regardless of how aware they are of that need. They are not meant to fight this problem on their own. Accountability is crucial to their fight for survival, because faith is not an isolated pursuit but is relationally driven. What effect are you having on a struggler? You will either help or hurt her sin struggles.

In this chapter, we'll look at nine characteristics of good accountability. Our goal is to help you to evaluate your efforts and see which areas of your accountability need improvement.

GOOD ACCOUNTABILITY IS TOUGH

Accountability serves a struggler well if it presses into his life and roots out his sin. These intrusive conversations are tough. The vulnerability that they require is hard because fear, shame, and guilt motivate the struggler to hide his sin and not expose himself. It's incredibly uncomfortable for a person to let others take a hard look at his sin. Yet vulnerability is necessary for survival. It exposes the ugliness of the sin as well as all the fears, despair, heartache, and messiness that surround it.

Superficial relationships don't root out sin and build hope. You need to go deep, even when it's tough. As the accountability partner, are you willing to ask hard, awkward, and direct questions? "Did you masturbate this week?" "Did you lie to anyone this week?" "Is there anything you are hiding from me?" Make sure you are not presuming you know all the right questions. The struggler knows his heart better than anyone else. Ask him, "Am I missing something? What else should I ask?"

You can ask tough questions all day long, but if your friend isn't honest and vulnerable with you, you are wasting your time. If strugglers are hiding things, not sharing the entire truth, or, even worse, lying to you, they undermine your ability to help. For accountability to work, the struggler has to be willing to respond to your tough questions with brutal honesty.

This means that even as you are tough in your accountability, you should do everything you can to celebrate and encourage honest responses from your friend. I (Deepak) had a friend call me the other

78

day and share with me that he'd fallen back into sexual sin and was viewing porn. My immediate response was, "I really appreciate how honest you are being with me about some very difficult struggles in your life." I affirmed his honesty because I know that's what God wants—that my friend would not hide but bring his sin into the light (see Prov. 28:13).

Take a risk—ask your friend about the nitty-gritty, ugly details of his life. Ask about the foulest parts of his heart. His sin will naturally push against this, wanting him to conceal or deny them, but redemption will beckon him to be truthful in all his ways. Solomon states, "An honest answer is like a kiss on the lips" (Prov. 24:26 NIV). Just as a kiss is delightful, so also is honesty.

GOOD ACCOUNTABILITY IS CONSISTENT

Good, consistent accountability is frequent and reliable.

Frequent help is better than infrequent help. Inconsistent accountability shows up occasionally but not often enough. Sin daily finds ways to muck up a struggler's life. If he lets it go unchecked for too long, it makes a mess of things. Your friend needs your repeated assistance in order to slow down and prevent the mess.

And when an accountability person does show up, he needs to follow through with what he has promised. For example, if you get filter reports, do you contact the struggler when something unhelpful shows up? If you don't, you're being unreliable. Because porn struggles are wreaking havoc in his life, a struggler needs help that is regular and reliable.

GOOD ACCOUNTABILITY IS LOCAL

Local accountability is much more useful than distant accountability. Often we'll ask a struggler, "Who is your accountability partner?" and she'll respond, "So-and-so, who is a good friend from a few years ago, when I lived in a different part of the country, still checks on me." Having someone who can check on the porn struggler only via technology (email, text, video call, and so on) is not ideal. At best, this kind of accountability offers only a slice of the struggler's life rather than a look at his entire life. Relationships that are sustained through technology are limited in their scope.

In the year 2020, we endured a worldwide pandemic, during which many people isolated themselves and relied on technology to communicate with their friends and family and even to participate in church services. As people began to share life together again, we saw the joy with which the members of our congregations returned to church, hugged one another, and spent time in one another's presence.

God could have left Adam alone with the animals in the garden of Eden, but he didn't (see Gen. 2:19–25). He gave Adam a partner (Eve) who was personally present with him throughout his life. Jesus didn't stay in heaven but came to earth to dwell among us and be personally present with us (see John 1:14; Phil. 2:7–8). And we see that the apostle Paul often yearned to be with his fellow believers, especially when he was locked up in prison (see Rom. 1:11; Phil. 1:8, 4:1; 1 Thess. 3:6; 2 Tim. 1:4).

These things show us that God has designed us, as image bearers, to give the most effective help when we are *personally present* in other people's lives. The most powerful way for you to give and receive accountability is for you to be regularly involved in someone's life. This way, rather than share a few words with an image on a screen, you get to enjoy life with the person you are discipling. You can sit across the table from your friend. Sit next to her in church. Go out to lunch with her. Go for a run with her. Give her a hug. Laugh together. Search the Scriptures and pray together. All this is possible when two people live geographically close to each other.

If you aren't able to provide local accountability for your friend, can you help your friend to find someone who is?

GOOD ACCOUNTABILITY IS COMMUNAL

Pursuing local accountability is not just about finding folks in close proximity to the struggler but about teaching the struggler to turn to an entire gospel community for help. John Freeman says, "We need a community to help us process our soul's discouraging elements and learn how to live a life of faith and repentance."[1] Thus the struggler needs godly friends who go to her church.

But why a church? Why can't the struggler just figure this out with one friend and leave it at that? Consider three reasons.

- The Lord tells us that his manifold wisdom is displayed through local churches (see Eph. 3:10). If that is God's plan, we want to be a part of it! We want to root our accountability in a gospel community.
- Scripture tells us there is more success with many counselors (see Prov. 11:14; 24:6) than with one.
- It's not good for the pressure and burdens of accountability to fall on one person's shoulders. Especially when things get difficult for the struggler, the situation may be a lot for the discipler or close friend to bear alone. Ideally, several people together will carry the weight of the struggler's problems, working as a team to care for their friend. This is something churches are designed to do (see Gal. 6:2; Heb. 10:24–25).

So if someone says, "I'm not sure who I should tell," we respond, "How about someone at church? A small-group leader? A godly discipler? A few of your closest friends at church? And, most importantly, your pastor?"

We all have concentric circles of relationships. Those in the inner circle are our most intimate friends. The further out we go into the concentric circles, the more superficial the relationships get. A struggler tells a few folks from his or her inner circle—a pastor, a small-group leader, a few close friends, and a discipler. It's normal for the struggler and the discipler to meet up. But what if the small-group leader or pastor occasionally shows up too? They talk, pray, and press in at the same time, working together for the spiritual well-being of the struggler. That way, they all get on the same page about what's wisest and best in the struggler's fight against sin and striving for faith.

It's vital that the struggler's pastor (or someone else in spiritual leadership) know about his plight. Leaders can't lead out of ignorance. If they don't know, they can't shepherd a lost, struggling, and feeble sheep. Make sure the struggler has told his pastor about his struggle.

GOOD ACCOUNTABILITY IS MATURE

Immature accountability is marked by a lack of wisdom. The apostle Paul describes the spiritually immature, who are worldly in their thinking, as infants who drink milk instead of eating solid food (see 1 Cor. 3:1–3; 14:20). All too often, a single person finds another single person who is fighting against sexual sin or a married person finds another married person who also struggles. That makes sense—a friend will understand what the struggler is going through (after all, he or she struggles with the same problem!). However, that friend likely won't have the aggressive disposition needed to help the struggler to fend off his or her sin (see Matt. 5:27–30).

Instead, accountability must be *mature*—a godly person who is loving, wise, and faithful, who is a season or two ahead of the struggler, and who doesn't wrestle with sexual sin. If you are a discipler, does that describe you? If not, where do you fall short? Listed below are criteria to help you to see if you are growing in spiritual maturity:[2]

- Do you hunger for God?
- Do you study God's Word such that you are growing in confidence in God and his promises? Is your life increasingly governed by Scripture?
- Do you pray and depend on the Lord for help?
- Are you committed to a local gospel-preaching church and modeling for younger believers what commitment looks like? Have you grown more concerned about the needs of others?
- Have you become more loving?

- Do you grieve over your sin? Are you quick to forgive? Have you learned to apply the gospel to your sin and suffering?

After reading these questions, you might think, "I fall far short. I'm not ready." If that's you, it's good to humbly admit such a thing and then help your friend to find a godly person who is ready to take on this responsibility. (If you are not sure what to think, then consult with your pastor or a wise Christian in your church.) Don't be surprised if a godly person's study of the Word and life experience make her well of wisdom much deeper.

GOOD ACCOUNTABILITY IS BROAD

Accountability must be placed in a larger framework of Christian friendship rather than restricted to the topic of fighting the sin of pornography. A relationship quickly becomes static if it is built solely on checking on sexual struggles. Your friend wants help with fighting his lust, but he needs much more: hope for daily struggles, more honest relationships with godly believers, and instruction on applying the gospel to the different aspects of his life. Accountability for sexual sin is just one component of his growth in Christ, and good accountability acknowledges that.

GOOD ACCOUNTABILITY IS GRACIOUS

A gracious attitude is essential for good accountability. You need to encourage the hopeless believer, show kindness to the fool, and love the struggler who has failed for the third time in a week. Remember, it's God's kindness that leads a sinner to repentance. If God is kind, shouldn't you be too? Don't be harsh and demanding, evoking the law often and displaying little of God's grace.[3] God is the final judge, and he has already forgiven the struggler in Christ. If you act like you, rather than God, are the ultimate judge, repent of that attitude.[4]

GOOD ACCOUNTABILITY IS FAITH-FOCUSED

Anyone can spend a lot of time focused on the horizontal dimensions of life—building friendships, paying bills, exercising, eating well, working hard, helping a neighbor—and lose sight of the vertical. Don't lose sight of faith. Faith in Christ is the chief goal.

When I (Jonathan) was meeting with Mateo, I knew he was discouraged because of his repeated falls over the last few weeks. We talked about the tactics of shutting down access to the Internet, not staying up late but getting to bed early, and rebuilding friendships in his church community. But I knew I shouldn't let him go without talking about Christ. So I asked him, "How does your faith make a difference in the fight against sexual sin?" Over the next few minutes, we had a fruitful conversation about how Mateo wanted to grow in greater trust in Christ. He desired greater faith.

GOOD ACCOUNTABILITY IS WORD-BASED

It is the Word that revives a dead heart and brings life. If you find you are not bringing the Word into enough of your conversations, change course right now. Rather than talking about anything and everything but God's Word, commit to making your conversations Word-driven.

As you consider the strengths and weaknesses of your accountability style, remember that, in the end, a struggler needs to be willing to do the hard work of fighting sin and pursuing faith. If you are constantly tracking her down or pressuring her to take the next step, you should back off and talk about her lack of motivation. "Are you willing to do what it takes? And if not, why not?" Even the best accountability can't save an apathetic struggler. Only God can.

Wisdom will grow through tough, consistent, local, communal, mature, broad, gracious, faith-focused, and Word-based accountability. If this is not what you are offering to a struggler, you can change. Ask the Lord for help, and adjust your approach in your next few meetings.

Reflect: If you are not offering good accountability, how should you change? If you are not sure whether you are mature enough to be offering accountability to a porn addict, read over the list of requirements for elders and deacons in 1 Timothy 3 and Titus 1. These form a list of maturity markers for a Christian. Though no one is sinless, the struggler will be most helped by someone who is *more* mature than he or she is rather than *less* mature.

Act: Focus on one of the qualities of good accountability in each of your upcoming meetings, making sure you are making adjustments to puruse a more vibrant and helpful accountability.

8

BEING GOSPEL-FOCUSED

*Becoming a Christian doesn't just add
something to the old you; it creates a new you.
The risen Christ indwells you now, never to leave.*
—*Ray Ortlund,* The Gospel

*We were buried therefore with him by baptism into death,
in order that, just as Christ was raised from the dead by the glory
of the Father, we too might walk in newness of life.*
—*Romans 6:4*

The gospel is the good news that Jesus has died for our sins and
been raised again, so that we can be reconciled back to God (see
Isa. 53:4–6; John 3:16; 2 Cor. 5:21). This is the seed from which all
of Christianity springs forth, and it is a fountain of hope for every
struggler. The gospel should infuse everything we do.

Whenever you help a struggling Christian, there is always a danger that you will veer off course. Scripture describes a narrow path
we should stay on—a path that is Christ-centered and gospel-rich.
But our tendency is to sway back and forth between biblical, God-
exalting, faith-oriented counsel and man-centered, pragmatic, short-
sighted, selfish strategies. We may not even know it, but some of our
advice may be subtly (if not overtly) unbiblical.

Consider three potential hazards as you seek to follow the gospel
path.

PUSHING PERSONAL RESPONSIBILITY
TO THE EXCLUSION OF GRACE

There is no such thing as fighting sin passively. We don't wait for God to fix our sin problems. A struggler needs to take personal responsibility for fighting his sin. To climb out of a ditch, he must grab hold of the rope that is offered to him and pull himself out. He must do something about his problem. This is the "work out your own salvation" part of Philippians 2:12.

But there is no such thing as a successful white-knuckle approach. Strugglers may foolishly try to fight their porn addictions through their own strength, limited resources, and finite wisdom. But they can't overcome addictions by mere willpower. If you or they think self-driven resolve is enough, you're foolish.

God gives strugglers the strength to fight. He infuses their hearts with hope. He motivates them to move forward. His undeserved kindness is in the driver's seat. A gospel-focused fight against an addiction always starts with God's grace.

Luke was overrun with pornography and masturbation for many years. But by the time I (Deepak) had lunch with him, he had led a pure, porn-free life for at least five years. He was genuinely free from sexual sin, though he wisely maintained vigilance. As we reflected back for a few minutes on the hard years, I asked what had pulled him out of the ditch, and he said, "Things changed for the good when my life no longer revolved around my sexual sin but around God's grace."

Grace. It's all about God's grace.

We can push too much responsibility on the sinner. We can demand so much of him that he begins to believe the lie that if he is good enough, disciplined enough, and smart enough, he'll defeat his sexual sin. But that's a man-centered, not a gospel-grounded, approach to defeating sin. The fight always starts with God. It begins with his grace.

NARROWING YOUR FOCUS DOWN TO SIN TO
THE EXCLUSION OF FAITH IN JESUS

Often when strugglers are drowning in their sin, there is so much for disciplers to cover—access points, heart issues, shame and guilt, anger at God, a single person's disappointment over not being married, or a wife's hurt over her husband's sexual sin. We can quickly be overcome, and we can spend far too much time talking about sin, sin, and more sin. (It never seems to go away, does it?)

One of the classic mistakes in accountability is to focus so much on defeating sin that we talk about it 96.7 percent of the time and shortchange the conversations about faith. We need to fight sin and defeat it. But that's only half the battle.

Faith is the wind in the sails of a struggler. It's what helps her to move forward in her fight. If she has the right object for her faith—Christ—she will win. Have no doubt about it. Without faith, the believer will be like a boat that sits on calm waters without any wind pressing on its sails. There will be no forward motion in her life.

As a discipler, you need to strike a balance in your conversations. Are you talking just as much about hope and faith as you are strategizing about how to defeat sexual sin? We talk about closing up access points, maintaining vigilance with our eyes, wrestling with deep heart issues, and confronting shame, but we need to infuse all our conversations with faith.

Take a moment and think about your last two or three conversations with the struggler you are discipling. Were you speaking mostly about sin and very little about faith? What would it take for you to talk more about faith, hope, love, joy, and grace?

If you find yourself talking too frequently about sin, we've got two suggestions. First, pray regularly through a list of biblical themes. You should let Scripture inform and shape your prayers. This is a good habit for any believer. But an additional benefit is that these Bible-saturated prayers can prompt you to talk about these same themes with a struggler. It's not unusual for the topic of grace, faith, or love to come to our minds during a discipling meeting because we prayed about it earlier that same morning. Second, as you (the discipler) keep yourself in God's Word for your own personal edification, let the redemptive themes found in the biblical texts spill out into your care of a struggler. Like water from an overflowing cup, your devotional life—your prayers and Bible reading—can pour into your discipling of a struggler.

PUSHING OBLIGATION TO THE EXCLUSION OF HOLY-SPIRIT-DRIVEN CONVICTION

When Trent confessed his sexual sin to me (Jonathan), he admitted that he was being lazy. "I know there are things I can do to fight it, but I just haven't been doing them," he said, embarrassed by his own admission. There were simple steps he could take to cut off the sin—steps of the "cutting off the arm, gouging out the eye" variety—that would lead to immediate results. They wouldn't solve his problems, but they would be a good beginning.

Put Covenant Eyes on his phone.

Set restrictions on his phone, and give the administrative controls to someone else.

Talk about his struggle with his friends, and be willing to confess when he falls.

Get rid of his Internet browser.

Get rid of any apps with an embedded browser.

I could have said, "You don't have a choice. You *must* do this. I insist." Instead I said, "Jesus encourages you in Matthew 5 to cut off your hand if it causes you to sin. Here's what I suggest you do. I'll pray for God to give you strength." If you'd overheard my conversation with Trent, you would have heard my firm but loving tone.

I couldn't make Trent take these steps. I didn't want him to be driven by obligation—to think, "I don't have a choice. Jonathan's pressuring me to do this." Instead, I encouraged him to cut off his access points to sin and prayed that the Holy Spirit would work in Trent's heart and motivate him to take action. He checked in with me a day or two after he'd finished the to-do list we'd compiled.

Pressuring a sinner to fight his sin will backfire. The struggler's motivation to fight will be to please you, not to live in holiness or to please God. That won't work. To win this war, the struggler has to be driven by the conviction of the Holy Spirit. No amount of pleading, cajoling, obligating, or pressuring will do the trick. You are not the Holy Spirit, nor should you pretend to be. Let the Holy Spirit do his job, and you stick to yours.

Reflect: How gospel-focused is your discipling? Are you pushing too much responsibility on the struggler? Do you talk about God's grace enough? Do you need to do it more? Are you too focused on fighting the sin? Can you talk about faith more? Are you putting too much personal pressure on the struggler? Is there room for the Holy Spirit to work?

Act: Make it a priority to be more gospel-centered in your conversations. Just take the simple step of asking more often, "How does the gospel have relevance to what we are talking about today?"

9

DISCERNING FAKE REPENTANCE

Penance does not work because it is founded upon self-trust.
But repentance to life is fused with trust in Christ as the
all-sufficient mediator between God and man.
—C. John Miller, Repentance and 21st Century Man

Like a dog that returns to his vomit is a fool who repeats his folly.
—*Proverbs 26:11*

Jackson called and said, "I messed up again." As a discipler, I (Deepak) was getting frustrated with him. He often called *after* he gave in to temptation but never beforehand. And it happened so often that I wondered if Jackson really understood genuine repentance.

If a porn struggler doesn't get repentance, you're wasting your time. When discipling men and women, you must teach, reteach, and clarify repentance. When pornography has overrun a believer's life, when guilt and shame become a common part of the Christian's daily struggles, when lies and self-justifications dominate the struggler's thinking, it's far too easy to lose sight of genuine, heartfelt, biblical repentance. So start a conversation by saying, "Define what repentance is." You'll be surprised by some of the answers you get.

Let's define what repentance is not before we speak to what it is in the next chapter. What we don't want is religious fakery—someone thinking her repentance is genuine when in fact it is counterfeit. Fake repentance ultimately reveals that a struggler is relying on herself to save herself and not on God.[1]

To be successful in defeating porn, you as the discipler need to discern the things that repentance is *not*. Here are seven of them.

REPENTANCE IS NOT THE SAME AS CONFESSION

Augustine rightly said, "The confession of evil works is the first beginning of good works,"[2] but it is just that . . . a beginning! If a Christian confesses his sin to his spouse or accountability partner, that is a good initial step. Confession—an acknowledgment of the wrong done—is a part of repentance, but it's not the whole thing.

A guilt-ridden believer articulates words of contrition, but there's a real danger that that's all they are—mere words that don't reflect a heart that is motivated to change. Repentance is not a verbal acknowledgment only. A believer can't say sorry and then do nothing about it.

REPENTANCE IS NOT SAYING SORRY AND STILL REPEATEDLY COMMITTING SEXUAL SIN

Henry feels like a hypocrite. Each time he apologizes to his wife, he turns around and commits sexual sin all over again. His lies, self-justifications, and excuses for his sin allow him to continue in it. Like a fool that repeats his folly (see Prov. 26:11), he holds on tightly to his sin. His wife rightly questions the genuineness of his repentance.

Pornography strugglers contextualize and explain away their sin—whether they're blaming their pornography use on lack of intimacy with their spouses or long days of work and stress. Genuine repentance cannot coexist with self-justifications and excuse making.

REPENTANCE IS NOT MERE BEHAVIOR CHANGE

Behavior change alone is not sufficient. The struggler may put restrictions on his phone, text his friends, pray, read his Bible, and go to bed early. If he undertakes these acts—even the distinctly religious ones—without a changed heart, they are mere behavioral adjustments (see Joel 2:13). Obedience does matter, but it must be tied to a heart motivated by love for God. Behavior that is severed from a transformed heart results in rotten fruit (see Luke 6:43–45).

A white-knuckling approach is a struggler's attempt to defeat his slavery to sexual sin through his own brute strength and force of will. The struggler who does this is steeped in self-reliance, self-trust, and self-justification. This sinner—foolishly—is far too confident in his ability to get through the mess, relying on himself rather than Christ (see 2 Cor. 5:15).

REPENTANCE IS NOT A BAD FEELING

"I'm an idiot." Colleen often feels horrible after she looks at pornography. But her wretched feelings are not the equivalent of genuine repentance—they are a cheap imitation.

Does genuine repentance involve emotions such as sorrow? Of course. But the apostle Paul says that there is a distinct difference between worldly grief—for example, bad feelings about being caught in sin—and godly grief, when a sinner feels the weight of offending a holy God (see 2 Cor. 7:10). We'll look more at this difference in the next chapter.

Many sexual sin strugglers wait until they feel better before they read their Bibles or talk with accountability, trying to get some distance from their last instances of acting out. They are trying to put distance between themselves and the wretched feelings of guilt and shame that overrun them right after they look at pornography.

REPENTANCE IS NOT PARTIAL[3]

Angelo knows what he has to do to fight against his sin, but he doesn't do it. A combination of shame, fear, and anger at God slows him down. His efforts are half-hearted at best. He asks for accountability, but he doesn't read his Bible. He goes to church, but he never prays. He confesses to a roommate, but he never tells his pastor because he doesn't want him to be disappointed in him. In Caroline's case, the sin is still too alluring, and she isn't ready to completely let go of it. She does just enough to put on the appearance of fighting sin, when in fact she is secretly still coddling it. When strugglers leave their fortifications against sexual sin incomplete, they show that they have not embraced genuine repentance.

REPENTANCE IS NOT PENANCE

For many, repentance is tightly associated with penance. Penance is a work done by the offender in order for him to be made "good" again. A believer does good works in order to make himself feel better. For example, Juan has struggled with sexual sin for several years. On Saturday afternoons, he helps his wife out—not because he is repentant, but because he wants to earn God's favor and prove himself to his wife.

In Roman Catholic theology, penance is a sacrament in which the individual confesses to a priest and then performs various good works in order to merit the forgiveness of his or her sins. Catholic theologians misunderstand cause and effect. Do good works *cause* repentance? No! God himself grants repentance (see Ps. 51:10). Do good works *follow* repentance? Yes! (See Matt. 3:8; Luke 3:8.)

REPENTANCE IS NOT A ONE-TIME EVENT AT CONVERSION

Repentance is a necessary part of coming to faith in Jesus (see Mark 1:15), but it is also an integral part of the believer's daily life. Sinclair Ferguson writes, "[Repentance] is perpetual. . . . It means ongoing, dogged, persistent refusal to compromise with sin. . . . True repentance can never be reduced to a single act found only at the beginning of the Christian life. It arises in the context of our union with Jesus Christ; and since its goal is our restoration into the image of Christ, it involves the ongoing practical outworking of our union with Christ."[4] Believers sometimes think they must repent to become Christians but don't need to make repentance a part of their lives after conversion. Martin Luther corrects this misunderstanding in the first of his famous ninety-five theses: "The entire life of believers is to be one of repentance."

THE LIFE OF FAKE REPENTANCE

Now that we've seen all that repentance is not, let's review common repentance substitutes we often run into. Does the person you are helping approach repentance like this?

- He often says, "I'm sorry," but repeatedly falls back into his sin. These consistent falls indicate that he has not experienced genuine heart change.
- He says, "I messed up," yet he regularly lies to himself, self-justifies, and makes excuses for his sin. He blames his circumstances ("This is such a stressful job") or other people ("If she'd be more open to sex, I wouldn't have to do this!").
- She takes a white-knuckling approach to defeating her sin, fighting by her own strength. Rather than joy, peace, or hope, you see anxiety and self-condemnation in her life.
- He feels bad about what he's done. Yet he's not concerned about offending God.
- His attempts to "repent" are half-hearted and partial. He offers an incomplete apology or takes only a few steps to stop sinning.
- She attempts to make up for her sexual sin by doing good deeds.
- He reduces his repentance to his conversion event but doesn't evidence a life of ongoing repentance.

Consider a complete profile of what fake repentance looks like. Let's think about Karl, someone who has struggled with pornography for many years. He doesn't daily repent but relies on himself to battle sexual sin. He listens to the false promises of sin rather than

God's Word. He buys into self-justifications for continuing to look at pornography. He's miserable and at times wallows in self-pity, depression, or disappointment. He does not experience a clear conscience, only an ongoing cycle of guilt and shame. He confesses, "This was bad," but keeps returning to his sin. Karl trusts himself more than he trusts God to get him out of his mess. He is sad over being caught or disappointed over what he will lose.

As you read this, you get a glimpse of the insanity of sin and the foolishness that drowns a porn struggler. Karl might say, "I'm sorry," yet, as you look at his entire life (which is filled with self-justifications, self-pity, depression, disappointment, cycles of guilt and shame), you see that his supposed repentance is really *not* repentance.

A key skill of a discipler is discerning counterfeits and helping the struggler to know when his repentance is illegitimate. If you notice any of these repentance substitutes in the life of your friend, it behooves you to speak up and confront him. Imagine yourself saying, "What you are doing is *not* repentance." The struggler's self-deception sets him up for more failure, so you *must* say something.

What great need there is for a Savior to rescue Karl! How deeply we need him to give disciplers the gift of discernment and strugglers the gift of genuine repentance. That's where we turn next.

Reflect: Do you recognize any of the repentance substitutes? Does the person you are helping hold to any of the false beliefs about repentance that we described in this chapter?

Act: If you are not sure whether the person you are helping is genuinely repentant, pray about it and write out what you see and notice in him. Sometimes writing things down helps to make them more clear.

10

ENCOURAGING GENUINE REPENTANCE

*Biblical repentance, then, is not merely a sense of regret
that leaves us where it found us. It is a radical reversal . . .
creating in us a completely different mind-set.*
—Sinclair Ferguson, The Grace of Repentance

*For godly grief produces a repentance that leads to salvation
without regret, whereas worldly grief produces death. For see what
earnestness this godly grief has produced in you, but also what
eagerness to clear yourselves, what indignation, what fear,
what longing, what zeal, what punishment! At every point you
have proved yourselves innocent in the matter.*
—2 Corinthians 7:10–11

In the last chapter, we considered what repentance is *not*, and we told
you about Karl, who is faking his repentance. Our friend Logan is
also struggling with sexual sin. How do we tell whether Logan is any
different from Karl?

In this chapter we'll examine what genuine repentance looks like.
We'll take two steps. First, we'll consider 2 Corinthians 7:8–11, a key
biblical text on repentance. Second, we'll consider what we know
about repentance from the totality of Scripture.

WORLDLY OR GODLY SORROW?

Here's the context for 2 Corinthians 7:8–11, our key text on
repentance. There was some kind of moral crisis in the Corinthian

99

church, most likely sexual sin (see 1 Cor. 6:14–7:1), and the congregation failed to support Paul in his work of discipling the offender among them. Paul sent the church a severe letter to confront them about their foolishness (see 2 Cor. 2:4; 7:8). The Corinthians' tolerance of sexual sin strained their relationship with the apostle and put it in peril.[1]

We see in our passage that initially Paul regretted chastising the Corinthian believers because his letter caused them grief. But the apostle's regret lasted only a little while before turning to joy. He saw that the Corinthians' grief was a *godly* grief that had turned into repentance. That repentance in turn led to salvation without regret.

The word *salvation* in 2 Corinthians 7:10 may refer to redemption in daily living and community life (see 2 Cor. 1:6; Phil. 2:12). But it's more likely that *salvation* refers to ultimate salvation, on the last day, when all men's works will be measured up based on the foundation they built their life on—whether Jesus Christ or other things (see 1 Cor. 3:10–15).

A contrite spirit is a necessary precursor to our repentance. (If a struggler isn't broken over his or her sin, you should be suspicious.) But the sorrow Paul is describing isn't just a person's bad feeling about being caught. Rather, it's *godly* sorrow—a sorrow that God works in the heart of a believer.[2] As the Spirit brings conviction, sin becomes appalling to the Christian rather than enjoyable. Instead of being concerned about getting caught, the sinner grieves his sin and its offense against God and others. This godly grief kindles repentance.[3]

Contrast this with worldly grief, which produces no repentance and leads to death and regret (see 2 Cor. 7:10). Worldly sorrow doesn't bring repentance because it has nothing to do with God—it is fundamentally selfish and revolves around worldliness. When we cut God out of the equation, all we have left to be concerned about is ourselves and the world we live in.

If you juxtapose godly and worldly sorrow, as Paul did, the

contrast creates a distinct way to measure up the porn struggler. What are you seeing? A brokenness before God or just guilty feelings? Does the sinner talk about how she's grieved God, or is she wallowing in self-pity? Is he experiencing a growing hope as he fights sin, or is he merely disappointed, depressed, and frustrated? Is the struggler zealous to do the right thing, or is she downplaying the concerns and integrity of the people who are most affected by her sin?

Godly grief should be evident in a genuinely repentant sinner.[4] In 2 Corinthians 7:11, Paul lays out seven different characteristics of godly grief and its fruit.[5]

Godly Grief Is Earnest

A person may experience worldly sorrow because of the unpleasant consequences of his sin, but he is apathic, careless, or indifferent when it comes to sin itself. For example, Mike is far more concerned about his wife's anger than his porn habit. His effort to clean up his act is driven by his fear of her, not by any Holy-Spirit-driven conviction about his sin. In contrast, consider Lee, who feels the weight of his sin before the Lord and is driven by it to make changes. A person who experiences godly sorrow is eager to deal with his problem. He takes radical steps to cut out the sin and get help.[6] He's desperate for the Word and aggressively pursues God. A newfound sobriety about the Lord shifts this sinner's perspective. He now agrees with God about who he is—a fool—and about the evil of what he's done.

What priority does repentance have in the daily life of the struggler you are working with? Is it an afterthought? Is repentance something that he will "get around to"?

Godly Grief Involves Eagerness to Clear Oneself

Worldly sorrow defends itself and makes excuses. Godly sorrow is eager to get rid of not only the sin but also the shame and stigma of the sin through repentance. Is the porn struggler comfortable with sin, allowing it to flourish and grow in her life without addressing it? Or is she eager to have herself vindicated from even the taint of sin through repentance?

Godly Grief Leads to Indignation

Worldly sorrow does not dissuade the sinner from coddling and embracing sin. Godly sorrow involves a righteous anger at the sexual sin. It is rightly indignant when this sin crops up. Out of their godly grief, the Corinthians no longer tolerated the offender's sin but felt righteous anger toward him. Is the sexual sinner indignant enough at his sin to stand up and cry out to God for rescue?

Godly Grief Fears God

Worldly sorrow is fed by a person's fear of getting caught with the sin. It's so scared that it hides from others. Godly sorrow is pre-occupied with an awe of and reverence for the Lord. It causes the struggler to talk about her sin as an offense against God and eagerly pursue anything that helps her to restore her relationship with the Lord. Is God the chief concern of the sinner you are helping? Or is he preoccupied with the bad fruit and messes created by his sin?

Godly Grief Is Filled with Longing and Zeal

The Corinthians' yearning and zeal were for their relationship with Paul to be restored. A person with worldly sorrow is more pre-occupied with earthly things (he is anxious about his life) or worldly concerns (he feels godless grief). That leaves him vulnerable to being tempted by selfish longings—he prioritizes lust and pleasure over and above healthy relationships. I (Deepak) counseled Helen, who didn't know what to do with the pain that accompanied her grief on the anniversary of her sister's death. In her sorrow, she turned to lustful pleasure as a comfort and refuge. Godly sorrow is accompanied by desires for holy things—for God, for his Word, for a restored relationship with those who have been hurt by sexual sin.

Godly Grief Accepts Punishment

Worldly sorrow is concerned with self-protection—with getting out of consequences and avoiding punishment. Godly sorrow prioritizes seeing justice done—righting any wrongs committed, providing restitution for damage that has been caused, and reconciling and repairing relationships that have been broken by sin.

In the last chapter we talked about Karl. Meeting Karl for the first time, you may not be able to tell if he is genuinely repentant, but if you begin to dig below the surface and press into his life, you'll start to notice some of the differences between his worldly sorrow and godly sorrow. Karl has a myopic focus—his attention is on himself, not on God. He doesn't care that he has offended the Lord or that his sin has affected others. He has not experienced lasting heart change. His contrition has a short timetable. His misery brings heartache and self-pity. He hides his sin, defends himself, and runs away from consequences.

Contrast Karl with Logan. Logan is broken over his sin. He is grieved that he has offended God and hurt his spouse. He cherishes God's forgiveness. In light of Logan's years of sexual sin, God's mercy is sweet to him. Disgusted by his sin, he is desperate to know Christ. God has changed his heart—he is eager for time in the Word and for fellowship with believers and accountability, and he is actively pursuing obedience. Surprisingly, he is experiencing bursts of joy he hasn't felt before.

On the surface, Karl's and Logan's sorrow might look the same, but when you dig deeper, you find that their relationships with God and the conditions of their hearts are fundamentally different. Which one of these men looks more like a Christian? Which man is experiencing worldly sorrow rather than godly sorrow?

Karl is on the fast track to death. Logan demonstrates "repentance that leads to life" (Acts 11:18). God did this. He took a wretched sinner and gave him the gift of repentance, and things changed. God humbled Logan and gave him a greater sense of his sin. Desperate for help outside himself, Logan ran to God, and the entire quality of his life was made new.

WHAT THE REST OF SCRIPTURE TEACHES US ABOUT REPENTANCE

Second Corinthians 7 is a helpful text for understanding genuine repentance, isn't it? Let's add to our knowledge by considering several more defining markers of repentance in Scripture.

Repentance Is God's Gift

Repentance is a gift of God's grace, as the Spirit quickens the conscience of the sinner over the wrong he or she has done. In another instance, Paul writes, "*God* may perhaps *grant* them repentance leading to a knowledge of the truth, and they may come to their senses" (2 Tim. 2:25–26). God brings about this repentance, not us.

No amount of self-will or self-determination can conjure up conviction of sin. David says in Psalm 51:10, "Create in me a clean heart, O God, and renew a right spirit within me." He recognizes his repentance is not self-generated, so he cries out to God, pleading for the Lord to change his heart.

A sinner can turn away from his folly for a time, but, absent true faith, his efforts are nothing more than works of the flesh. Without faith, they won't last. True repentance is a product of genuine faith. Like the father who cried out, "Help my unbelief!" (Mark 9:24), the sinner must turn to Christ. Kelly Needham points out, "Repentance isn't primarily about *what* you're fleeing from but *whom* you're fleeing to. What good is it to run from sin if you're running to your own resources?"[7]

"Repentance will always come *from* faith. It is a byproduct of faith. It is an overflow of faith. Where faith is, *there* repentance will necessarily be. Thus, where faith is produced, or where faith is grown, repentance will naturally flow." **—Charles Hedman**[8]

Repentance Is Motivated by God's Holiness, Forgiveness, and Abundant Kindness

In the light of God's holiness—his sinless perfection—a believer fears and trembles before the Lord. How can a sinner stand before a holy God (see Isa. 6:5)? He can't. When we speak of fear, we're typically thinking of the fear of spiders or mean people or standing at the top of a skyscraper and looking downward. But fear in the Bible is a reverence and awe of the Lord. Bryan Chapell writes,

"True repentance starts with recognition of the holiness of our God."[9] When a porn struggler recognizes his sin in light of God's holiness, his heart and life begin to change. He sees that his sin is against God first and foremost, not others.

King David came to understand this after the prophet Nathan confronted him. He prayed, "Against you, you only, have I sinned and done what is evil in your sight, so that you may be justified in your words and blameless in your judgment" (Ps. 51:4). Dominic was so caught up in how he hurt his wife that he lost sight of the fact that his sin was first an offense against God. As he repented, his prayer was "Lord, help me to be more ashamed of how I have betrayed you."

To be motivated by a fear of God is good, but we need to be motivated by more. Forgiveness is one of the sweetest parts of Christianity. As the sinner repents, his hope is in a loving and forgiving God who waits for him with open arms (see Luke 15:20–21; 1 John 1:9). Sinclair Ferguson writes, "Repentance is possible because of the great promise of forgiveness."[10] When we turn to God in authentic repentance, we can rest assured that the Lord's pardon is full, free, and immediate.

God is kind and forbearing with sinners (see Rom. 2:4). A sinner responds to God's kindness because she knows it is not deserved. She knows she's unworthy of God's love, mercy, and forbearance, and that motivates her to repent and return to the Lord. He could send us to hell immediately, but he does not. He patiently waits for us, for it is his kindness that leads us to repentance. "The Lord is not slow to fulfill his promise as some count slowness, but is patient toward you, not wishing that any should perish, but that all should reach repentance" (2 Peter 3:9).

Repentance Is a Turn–Away from Our Sin and to Christ

The penitent turns his back on sin, renouncing it and saying, "I don't want it anymore!" He's disgusted with his sin. It leaves a bitter taste in his mouth. As a sexual sinner rejects his sin and turns away from it, he turns to his Savior, and with his whole life he runs to him. There is a turn—a distinct change of direction.

Malachi 3:7 says, "Return to me, and I will return to you, says the Lord of hosts." God makes a promise—if we return to him, he will come toward us. Think of the Prodigal Son who came to his senses and went back to his father in Luke 15:17–20. From a long way off, his father saw him. Filled with compassion, he ran to his son and embraced and kissed him.

Turning away from our sin and toward Christ means turning away from ourselves (see 2 Cor. 5:15). We should never be the focus of our repentance—spending our time mentally berating ourselves or feeling bad about ourselves. Heath Lambert writes,

> Mental punishments are not helpful because they deal with sin in a self-centered way instead of a Christ-centered way. Meditating on how miserable and pathetic you are only perpetuates the sinful self-centeredness that led you to look at pornography in the first place. Condemning self-talk still has *you* standing center stage as *you* reflect on what *you* think about what *you* have done, and as *you* describe what *you* think *you* deserve because of what *you* did. It's all about *you*. The problem is there is too much *you* in all this. *You* need *Christ*. And the only way to break the vicious cycle is to get outside of yourself to Jesus.[11]

All true repentance involves not only turning *from* one's sin and *from* one's self but turning *to* Christ in faith.

Repentance Is an Inner Heart Change That Leads to Greater Obedience

A change of heart leads to a change of life. The repentant struggler increasingly leaves behind old habits and desires. An offended party, such as a betrayed spouse, may experience heartache, but the sexual sinner no longer regrets the sin she has committed (see 2 Cor. 7:10). Instead she experiences a newfound relishing of God's mercy. Filled with new convictions, the repentant sinner sets a new direction for her life and makes better, wiser, and more godly choices ("fruit") that are in keeping with her repentance (see Matt. 3:8; Acts 26:20). Her obedience is motivated by a love for God, a conviction of sin, and a desire to be known (see Eph. 5:8–10).

Repentance Leads to Zealously Cutting Off All Sin

A repentant sinner takes a zealous approach to eliminating sin. He heeds Christ and the Spirit's exhortation: "Be zealous and repent" (Rev. 3:19). Hence, he is proactive in dealing with temptation when it shows itself and aggressive in fighting his sin after a fall.

Repentance Leads to a Newfound Humility

Pride or self-reliance, acceptance of the false promises of sin, and self-condemnation all result in the sinner's attempting to fight on her own. Pride messes her up. And we know the warning of Scripture: "God opposes the proud but gives grace to the humble" (James 4:6). Genuinely repentant sinners are humble. If they do fall to temptation, they quickly get help. In humility, they recognize that they desperately need others. They aggressively seek out accountability and welcome rebuke (see Prov. 15:31; 17:10). Humility overrules pride and fear of man. It's honest and willing to say embarrassing things for the sake of holiness. It takes initiative to bring sin to the light. It prefers transparency, vulnerability, and a life in the light over shame, darkness, and hiding (see Eph. 5:3–13).

Repentance Leads to Rectifying Wrongs and Making Amends

Sinners take responsibility for their wrongdoing (see Luke 19:1–10). They recognize the damage they have done. They know the pain they have caused loved ones and take responsibility for it rather than blaming others. They don't minimize or downplay their wrong.[12] Rather, they proactively make restitution.

When John's wife catches him watching porn, he doesn't blame her or excuse his sin by pointing to how stressed he's been. Rather, he wholeheartedly accepts the wrong he's done. The very next day, he puts Covenant Eyes on his phone and laptop and confesses to his accountability partner. He wants to take active steps to prevent his sin. When he stumbles a few weeks later, he immediately goes to his wife and accountability partner and confesses. He wants to show his wife that he will be quick to confess sin and rectify his wrongdoing. He emphasizes his care and his dedication to rebuilding trust with his wife by being extra attentive and servant-hearted in the following week.

Repentance Leads to Accepting Consequences for Sin

Piet messes up by looking at porn yet again, but he doesn't want his wife to restrict his Internet access. Once she says, "I forgive you," he assumes they can move on and leave the issue in the rearview mirror. When she asks to see his phone or insists on greater transparency, he balks at her requests. "You said you forgive me, so why can't we just forgive and forget?" he angrily demands. "Why do you keep bringing this up?"

Like other Christians we've met, Piet thinks things will get better after he "repents." He thinks confessing his sin will remove certain consequences of that sin. But the aftermath of sexual sin is often ugly, messy, and difficult to navigate. Much of that mess does not disappear simply because the sinner "repents."

A believer who superficially (and falsely) repents will do the initial work of prayer and confession but be unwilling to bear consequences for his sinful actions. Bryan Chapell writes, "True repentance . . . willingly accepts [the consequences] if they move us closer to fellowship with and understanding of our God."[13]

Genuinely repentant sinners do whatever is needed to make things right (see Luke 23:40–41). They are patient with those whom they have offended. They are willing to be transparent, make sacrifices, lose friends, quit jobs, offer restitution, and end relationships. They don't demand to be forgiven or treated a certain way. They show patience toward the people they have hurt by their sin, knowing they will need time to heal and work through the hurt. They are willing to be inconvenienced, especially if it helps out the offended party.

Repentance Is Ultimately Centered around a Joyfully Restored Relationship with God

The goal of biblical repentance is a joyfully restored relationship with God. Chapell says, "Repentance renews our joy."[14] David attests to this as well in Psalm 51. The central point of this psalm of repentance is found in verse 12: "Restore to me the joy of your salvation, and uphold me with a willing spirit."[15] One way we assess the authenticity of a person's repentance is by observing whether or not joy is present. There is no morbid introspection—no moping around, no seeking pity from others. No, repentance revels and takes joy in a restored relationship and communion with God. The repenter can exult in the following words from David:

> Blessed is the one whose transgression is forgiven,
>   whose sin is covered.
> Blessed is the man against whom the LORD counts no iniquity,
>   and in whose spirit there is no deceit. (Ps. 32:1–2)

One who truly repents takes joy in his forgiveness, understanding that the basis of his renewed right standing with the Father is the sacrificial work of Jesus Christ.

> Grant me never to lose sight of
>   the exceeding sinfulness of sin,
>   the exceeding righteousness of salvation,
>   the exceeding glory of Christ,
>   the exceeding beauty of holiness,
>   the exceeding wonder of grace.[16]

Reflect: As a discipler, what do you see in the struggler—godly or worldly sorrow? Is the struggler hoping in God or running away from him? Is he pursuing greater obedience, or is he ashamed and hiding? Is he willing to sacrifice for the offended party, or is he unwilling to face the consequences of his sin?

Act: Pray that the Lord would grant repentance to sexual sinners in your life. Plead for God's mercy on their behalf. Then go to your struggling friends and lovingly exhort them to turn to Christ.

11

TAKING A WIDER GAZE AT SIN

It's very important . . . not to let the high-profile
wrongs [prevent] us from seeing the whole picture.
—David Powlison, Making All Things New

And let us not grow weary of doing good,
for in due season we will reap, if we do not give up.
—Galatians 6:9

Brandon berated his wife in front of me. He and Gloria had stopped in for a marital counseling session. I (Deepak) was surprised that he was so harsh, since they had been doing well over the past few months. When I confronted Brandon about his behavior, the conversation deteriorated. (Not every counseling story goes well!)

About a week later, Brandon called to let me know he was struggling with pornography. I kicked myself. I can't tell you how often I see prideful and self-righteous behavior in fellow church members, only to find out later that they've also been struggling with pornography. Coincidence? Not at all.

MEET THE TREE

The Bible often uses agricultural metaphors to describe human beings (see, for example, Ps. 1; Jer. 17:1–13). We first encountered the image of the tree in chapter 2. The *roots* of this tree are a person's spiritual heart—the central and most core part of who he is as an image bearer (see Prov. 4:23; 27:19). The *fruit* of this tree is what

111

flows out of his heart (see Matt. 12:34–35; Luke 6:43–45). Scripture tells us that out of the overflow of our hearts we act, think, and speak. Bad roots and poor conditions result in a tree full of rotten fruit—and, in the same way, sins of the heart and the red-hot heat of difficulties far too often yield the bad fruit of ungodly sexual habits.

TAKE A WIDER GAZE AT THE ROOTS

Sexual sin, like any other type of sin, typically does not flourish in isolation. It is rarely *just* sexual sin. Lust is seldom its only cause. Different roots all connect to the same tree—and pride, entitlement, boredom, fear, and anger can produce sexual sin just as much as lust does.

Nevertheless, far too often a porn struggler insists that lust is *The Problem* and has led to his pornography use and masturbation. He's tempted to offer simplistic explanations about his sexual sin struggles: "It's a lust problem . . . that's all." His simple view of sexual sin looks like this:

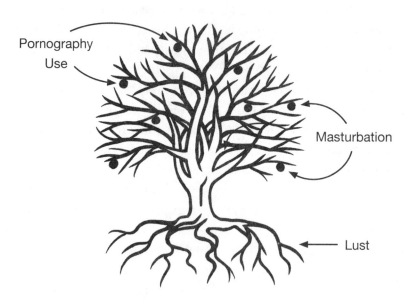

Fig. 11.1. A Simplistic View of Sexual Sin

"Counseling must always focus on specifics, because you can't talk about everything at once. When counseling tries to isolate one particular problem as The Problem, it loses the interconnectedness between many aspects of a person's life. Tunnel vision is not the way God goes about working in people. Often a tough, perplexing problem starts to yield when one of the 'connections' or 'underlying causes' or 'next door neighbor[s]' is brought onto the table. Seeing how wider and deeper problems connect to The Problem brings a great deal of hope. It lets counseling ministry aim for progress on many interrelated fronts, creating ripple effects. It makes counseling wonderfully flexible, surprising." —**David Powlison**[1]

Lust, masturbation, and pornography are *the* big scary sins that everyone wants to talk about, but in fact more sins are lurking if you look around. Some of these lesser actors are invisible to the struggler, and we serve him by bringing attention to the sins and struggles that hide in the shadows.[2]

Brandon's pride fueled his self-righteous attitude about his pornography struggles. He would think, "I got this" and "I don't need anyone else's help." It just took me (Deepak) a while to realize that the root of pride in Brandon's life was yielding *multiple* bad fruits— from a harsh attitude toward his wife to persistent sexual sin.

Of course, because of the interconnectedness of sin, we can't draw a direct line from the root of pride to the fruit of sexual sin. Usually multiple roots and heart issues combine and build on each other to produce bad fruit.[3] Not only was Brandon proud, he was also angry at God and his spouse, fearful of other people's opinions, and greedy for pleasure. Life is not simplistic. It's often messy and complicated.

A believer cannot repent of one area of sin (like lust) but cultivate other roots of sin on the side (like pride, selfishness, or anger). It's important to help him to see his struggle from a wider perspective. Is Brandon only repenting of lust? Or is there more? Have his heart and roots been infected by anger, selfishness, and pride? How can we help him to see *all* the bad roots of the tree, not just a few isolated ones?

TAKE A WIDER GAZE AT THE ENVIRONMENTAL CONDITIONS

Author and counselor John Henderson points out certain environmental conditions under which sexual sin will flourish.[4] To build on our tree illustration, certain bad environmental conditions (termites, a lack of nutrients or sunlight, toxic chemicals in the dirt) hurt a tree's roots and will likely lead it to produce bad fruit. In our lives, some examples of bad environments are stress, loss of control, worldliness, and nasty conflict.

An addict can't blame her circumstances—difficult situations don't cause her to sin. But circumstances are significant and influential in shaping her heart and life.

Stress

Anxiety is the outward manifestation of deeper fears surrounding some perceived danger. We experience anxiety as worry, stress, panic, nervousness, overwhelmed feelings, fretfulness, agitation, and apprehension. When a person is worried or stressed out, his heart and mind focus on some temporal thing that becomes a centerpiece of his life. He frets over something he might lose—maybe his health or safety or a material object. He gets preoccupied with another person's opinion or a job promotion that he is yet to be granted.

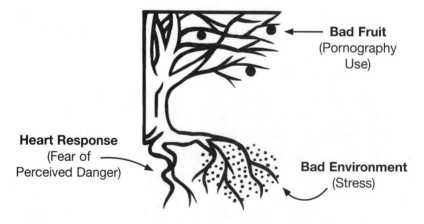

Fig. 11.2. Stress Leads to Pornography Use

When a struggler is anxious or stressed out, pornography acts as a powerful sedative for her worries. It helps to soothe her and temporarily assuages the fretfulness that comes when she spends too much energy on being preoccupied with the object of her worries. "It helps release physical tensions and calm agitated emotions. It enables us to avoid the root causes of our anxiety by quieting all the deafening noise of daily deadlines, expectations, and responsibilities."[5]

Loss of Control

Life offers many challenges—most of them mundane but occasionally some that are very difficult. It's not unusual for a porn struggler to avoid real life by fantasizing. Brandon would take images stored in his brain and turn them into a full-blown movie in which he was the hero of the story and surrounded by voluptuous women. When his life felt out of control, pornography created an alternate universe under his control. The most attractive women affirmed and desired him. Meanwhile, a struggling woman fantasizes that the most handsome and well-built men want to be with her and have sex with her. That's not real life. It's a fantasy. But with pornography, things feel under her control.[6]

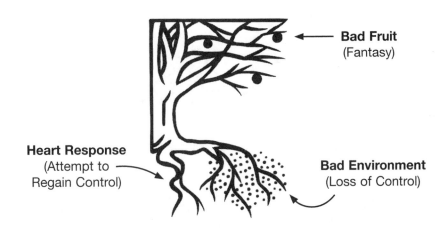

Fig. 11.3. Loss of Control Leads to Fantasy

Sensuality and Worldliness

A person's preoccupation with the world will only increase his desire for sexual sin. When television shows, reading material, music videos, and our culture as a whole are tainted with sensuality and sexual innuendo, it's hard for a porn struggler to maintain any semblance of purity. He's daily surrounded by sex. At the same time, the world preaches an anti-authority, do-whatever-you-want message, which encourages the freedom of sexual expression that is now the norm.

Sex is a wonderful gift from God. But illicit sensuality can overrun a believer's life. A good desire for sex and intimacy turns into a full-blown addiction as a Christian's ungodly desires are further fueled by sensuality and worldliness. These environmental conditions are like wood for an already burning fire. Exacerbated by these conditions, a struggler's greed for sexual sin turns into an all-consuming ungodly desire that overtakes her life.

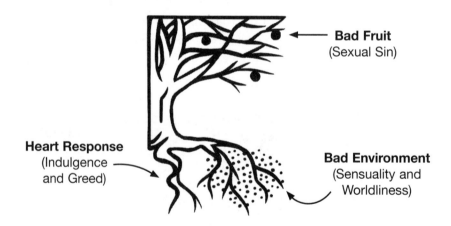

Fig. 11.4. Sensuality and Worldliness Leads to Sexual Sin

Conflict

A husband and wife argue for months. She berates him for pretty much everything. Meanwhile, an attractive coworker pays attention to the husband, flirts with him, and praises him often. With his home-life a warzone, the husband calls up the coworker after a nasty fight with his wife and asks her out to dinner. Their relationship quickly moves to an affair. What does his wife do when she finds out? She seduces her husband's best friend. Is sex involved? Sure. But sex is a mere weapon in the hands of an angry couple. Anger and a desire for vengeance can lead people to use sex to do harm rather than good.[7]

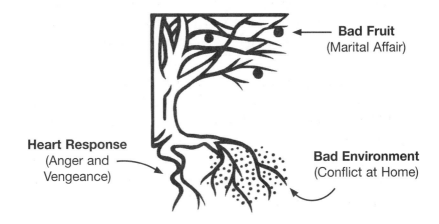

Fig. 11.5. Conflict at Home Leads to an Affair

TAKE A WIDER GAZE AT THE BAD FRUIT

Bright, juicy Golden Delicious apples are delightful to consume—but consider the disappointment of stumbling across an apple tree that yields only mushy, rotten apples. As we've seen, sexual sin is a bad fruit that stems from many damaged roots and unhealthy environments. Let's consider a few different kinds of rotten fruit that can emerge alongside sexual sin on a tree.

- *Shame and hiding.* Just as Adam and Eve ran and hid after they disobeyed God's command by partaking of the forbidden fruit (see Gen. 2–3), so porn strugglers hide from God and others. They cover themselves with fig leaves because they are embarrassed by their exposure. Brandon couldn't face up to his wife's anger, so he hid his sin for weeks, sometimes even months. He was too embarrassed to say something to her.

- *Deceit and lying.* Brandon covered his tracks by lying to hide his mistakes and folly. He figured, "What my wife doesn't know won't hurt her." He was wrong.
- *Escapism.* At the peak of his stress, Brandon would shut the door and plunge himself into pornography. It was his way of escaping his unbearable work conditions at the office.
- *Intoxication.* When Brandon's drive for sexual sin became a ruling desire in his life, his mind and heart became intoxicated. It was like he was under a spell. His every thought, feeling, and action became preoccupied with sexual sin. He saw everything through a sexual lens.[8] His whole life became oriented around attaining another sexual experience.
- *Dehumanization.* Pornography distorts an accurate perception of sexuality and beauty. Brandon didn't treat the porn stars he watched as valuable and dignified because they were made in God's image. Rather, he reduced them to the petty objects of his desires and pleasures. Sadly, his porn habit also led him to hold a dehumanizing view of the people he interacted with in real life, particularly his wife.

This is just the tip of the iceberg. The list of bad fruit yielded by porn addiction is endless: relational strife, impatience, loneliness, depression, disappointment, bitterness, and so on. We shouldn't be surprised.

Think in terms of the principle of sowing and reaping: "For whatever one sows, that will he also reap" (Gal. 6:7). Ungodly motivations and heart issues sown eventually reap a harvest of useless, rotten fruit. That was Brandon's life. Imagine standing in front of a farmer, at the start of planting season, and handing him a bag of seeds labeled *pride, anger, fear,* and *foolishness.* When these seeds are planted, they will yield nothing but bad fruit—the low quality, mushy, cheap apples you get from the discount grocery stores. "For the one who sows to his own flesh will from the flesh reap corruption" (Gal. 6:8).

Reflect: Before you consider the root, fruit, and conditions of a porn struggler's life, reflect on your own life. What would you see if you drew a tree for yourself?

Act: Get the believer you are helping to draw his own tree and identify his environmental conditions, roots, and bad fruit. What motivates him to sin? If he is not sure, talk through a specific incident of temptation and falling, and you'll get plenty of specific data about his struggles. What is he missing that you need to fill in?

12

REVIVING A DEAD CONSCIENCE

Feeding excuses to your conscience is like
feeding sleeping pills to a watchdog.
—*Andrew David Naselli and J. D. Crowley,* Conscience

So I always take pains to have a
clear conscience toward both God and man.
—*Acts 24:16*

Brittany lives a lie. Her husband doesn't realize it, but she's been mired in sexual sin for a good portion of their marriage. She's worked hard to cover her tracks. He has a sense of it based on her suspicious behavior (though he never has access to her phone), the things she reads (steamy, sex-laden trash), gaps in their finances (which she oversees but never shows him), and times when he can't account for her. One day when he initiates sex, he can tell that although she is physically present, the rest of her is somewhere else. He finally has to ask, "What's wrong with us?" Their marriage has gone stale, worse than bread left out for months. Their cold and lifeless sex life is a sign of their marital problems.

Gerald started with pornography, but his sexual sin turned into carefully planned escapades in which he has sex with strangers. Several apps on his phone provide him with opportunities to engage in sex with random people. Pornography is the fuel that feeds his desires, and when the fire is stoked, he acts out by finding someone who will give him what he wants. If he can't find it via a planned hookup, he manipulates a woman he knows into a one-night stand.

121

The women mean nothing to him. Sex is his god. The women are just a means to an end—the way he tries to satisfy the sex-driven ruling desires of his heart.

Brittany and Gerald are churchgoers and professing believers. Gerald even leads a Bible study. On the inside, they are as dead as rotten wood. Hollow hearts. Fake lives. No affection for gospel truth or God's people. Their joy in Christian fellowship and in knowing the truth has vanished. They fake Christianity, having lost their hearts for God and no longer giving their lives to their loved ones. What has happened? How did they get to this point?

If you get below the hood, you can see why your car sits immobile on the roadside, making noises that it shouldn't. If you lift the hood of a porn struggler, you'll see why things have gone so wrong. Fuel leak? Malfunctioning sensors? Water damage? Corroded battery? Much worse. Try a dead conscience. We don't need X-ray vision to see why Brittany and Gerald are doing so poorly and why their sin patterns have started to rule their lives. Their problems started when their consciences were weakened, then hardened, then eventually killed.

That's what we want to explain in this brief chapter—the plight of Brittany and Gerald's dead consciences and how best to revive them.

THE DEADLY TRIAD

A Dead Conscience

The conscience is a God-given capacity to distinguish between right and wrong. Because our God is a moral God, he gives those made in his image an ability, known as the conscience, to decipher morality.[1] If you grew up in a home in which your parents taught you the difference between right and wrong, it shaped your conscience. When you are converted, the Lord uses the common means of grace (Scripture, relationships with other believers, church attendance and participation) and the conviction of the Holy Spirit to further refine your conscience and give it a sense of right and wrong that lines up with God's definition of right and wrong.

Picture a believer's conscience as a circle, with a clear and distinct line that divides good from evil, right from wrong. Though sin attempts to make this less distinct, the Lord uses his Word, his people, and his Spirit to reform our consciences to look like his.

A struggler's repeated exposure to porn, ongoing acting out, and engagement with sexual sin corrupts her conscience. It's not just "defiled" (1 Cor. 8:7), guilty (see Heb. 10:22), and wounded (see 1 Cor. 8:12)—over time, it becomes weakened (see 1 Cor. 8:7, 10, 12).[2] As the conscience changes, the line becomes fuzzy and less distinct.

The first time a man or woman looks at porn, alarm bells go off in his conscience. It tells him, "No, don't do this. It's exciting, but it's wrong." But with time, as the struggler is regularly exposed to naked images and videos of sex, the alarm bells grow quieter. As warnings are ignored, they grow weaker. The roar turns into a whisper. The line between right and wrong grows blurry. A weakened conscience grows confused as what it once hated (sexual immorality) is now loved, and what it once loved (God) is now forgotten.

With enough time, the conscience's alarm bells grow silent. The conscience becomes hardened and callous (see 2 Cor. 8:10).[3] Like a smoke detector with uncharged batteries, it's still there, but it's lifeless and useless. Persist in sexual sin, and the conscience, in time, becomes seared (see 1 Tim. 4:2). Repeatedly using pornography is like using a sledgehammer on the smoke detector. It destroys the conscience. It no longer functions properly. It becomes inactive, silent, insensitive, and no longer responsive to sin.[4]

The believer has destroyed his conscience (see 1 Tim. 4:2). And this is *his* fault. We can't blame God or anyone else.

No Gospel Affections

As the conscience dies, the struggler's once-flourishing gospel affections get snuffed out. The believer's affections for Christ are dampened and eventually extinguished. The struggler no longer worships Christ. No one can see that her heart is overrun by distorted desires and ignores Christ rather than adoring him.

Ruling Carnal Desires

The death of a conscience allows a struggling believer's carnal desires to run amok. They overrun and rule her heart as she feeds her pornography habit. With her conscience dead and her gospel affections gone, the carnal, ruling desires are left to reorient the believer's life around wrong things—sex rather than God, selfishness rather than self-sacrifice and love, and sin's salacious promises rather than Christ.

This is the deadly triad: a deadened conscience, a loss of affections for Christ, and a life overrun by carnal, ruling desires. This triad is the irreducible core of a pornography addiction. It's what creates lifeless, sex-crazed human beings like Brittany and Gerald. The idolatry and foolishness of sexual sin that persists over the course of months and years turn believers into hollow versions of their former selves. These image bearers who are meant to glorify God and love others don't function as they should.

THE CONSEQUENCES OF A DEAD CONSCIENCE

Picture this scenario: You set up Internet monitoring software for Liam on his electronic devices. He's battled pornography for years, but he's never used this kind of software before. Initially, it's extremely helpful. He is deeply ashamed and can't bear the thought of your knowing or seeing what he looks at in his dark moments, so the monitoring software slows him down significantly. Although he feels the pull of pornography and tries to find workarounds on the software, he gives up because he can't figure out how to get around all the blocks on his computer. For the first few weeks, the accountability reports are all good.

However, one day Liam's wife, Juliet, leaves her laptop open and rushes out to the grocery store to buy a few things before dinner. Liam feels trapped. It's been weeks since he's had open, unmonitored access to the Internet. His wife's laptop is open and exposed. And she is twenty minutes away at the store. *"Now! Get it before she gets back!"* he thinks, already reaching for the laptop.

As with other believers who are overrun by and entrenched in porn, Liam experiences almost no length of time between thinking a sexualized thought and acting out. Why is that? Although his conscience has had a few weeks to attempt to revive, it's still essentially lifeless.

Prior to Liam's porn addiction, his conscience's divided line between good and evil was like the thick, impenetrable wall of a dam, holding back the water. However, Liam has spent years mired in pornography. Now that his conscience is dead, the dividing wall is gone, and there is nothing to hold back the carnal desires from wreaking havoc.

Have you ever wondered why a seemingly repentant sinner who gains temporary access to pornography jumps right at it without any hesitation? In Liam's case, godly values and morality no longer set the agenda for his life; his carnal desires do. In a brief moment of open access to Internet pornography, Liam reaches out and grabs all that his carnal desires and sexually crazed heart demand. With his conscience dead, Liam's carnal desires rule this moment. They demand, "More, more, more!" His in-the-moment thinking causes him to lose sight of any future consequences, like how angry and disappointed his wife will be when he has to confess his sin to her.

BREATHING LIFE BACK INTO A DEAD CONSCIENCE

Life comes back to dead consciences when strugglers look outside themselves. That's the most basic rhythm of gospel thinking: "I'm in trouble—I need help. I can't do this on my own." Faith revives a dead conscience. A struggling Christian can't fix her conscience on her own. However, God can. As the Holy Spirit revives faith and grants the gift of repentance, he also quickens a dead conscience. God comforts a troubled conscience, softens a calloused heart, and breathes life into a hopeless soul.

If my (Deepak's) Honda minivan's speedometer reads ten miles slower than the speed I'm actually driving, it does me no good when I'm pulled over by a police officer. "But, officer," I plead, "my speedometer is wrong." The officer doesn't care in the least. What matter are the miles per hour that registered on his speed gun.[5] I need to recalibrate my speedometer so it is accurate—and a discipler needs to help a calloused sinner to recalibrate his conscience. We offer three suggestions for doing so.

The Discipler Encourages Humility

The discipler must encourage humility. The struggler's dead conscience must come under the lordship of Christ.[6] Biblical truth directs him to what is right and wrong. He must submit his conscience to the Word of God, recalibrating it according to God's truth—the ultimate distinguisher of right and wrong, good and bad.

If a struggler knows her conscience is dead and not trustworthy, this may mean that for a time she needs to lean on the wisdom of others outside herself—a godly mentor and trusted leaders who live with clean consciences that are informed by God's Word. We've known plenty of men or women who, as they emerged from a darkened season, recognized that they couldn't trust themselves because their consciences were no longer reliable guides and their carnal desires were setting the agenda for their lives.[7] Our goal is to help such people to ignore the demands of their carnal desires and to trust others' consciences. This gives their dead consciences a chance to come back to life.

The Discipler Encourages Repentance, Faith, and Obedience

The discipler should encourage repentance, faith, and obedience in the struggler's life. Pornography has destroyed the struggler's conscience's ability to preserve moral order in his life. But there is hope. Consistent repentance and faith in Christ revive that ethical line of the believer's beleaguered conscience. As they make the line clearer and more distinct, the conscience regains its vitality and power.

Vertical repentance—repentance before God—is of utmost importance. Whenever a believer chooses to look at pornography, the moment is defined by unbelief and loss of God-consciousness. As carnal desires rule his heart, he ignores God and gets trapped in his tiny little kingdom, where his sin is all that matters. Through faith-driven repentance, his relationship with God is restored. In confessing his sin to God, the addict cultivates a right fear of God (see Ps. 34:11–14)—recognizing that his sin is ultimately an offense against a holy God (see Ps. 51:3–4)—that facilitates a right understanding of who God is according to the Scriptures. A right understanding of God is the first step in rebuilding the moral foundations for a dead conscience.

A struggler's every act of faith-driven repentance and every small step of obedience redeems his conscience a little bit at a time and puts to death the selfish desires of his sinful nature (see Gal. 5:24). The conscience's fuzzy line becomes more distinct, and the struggler's carnal desires slowly die. A thousand small steps of obedience rebuild Christian character and revive the conscience. Obedience matters. One antidote to a dead conscience and selfish desires is a daily habit of quick repentance and consistent obedience.

The Discipler Prays

We encourage humility, repentance, faith, and obedience because the struggler has a part to play in working out his sanctification. But we know that the conscience is ultimately revived by the Lord. Thus, our third suggestion is that the discipler pray and encourage the struggler to pray as well. The discipler asks, "Lord, breathe life into my friend's dead conscience and help him to see the beauty of Christ." The struggler prays, "I beg you, Lord, to help me and give me back a conscience that loves what you love."

Reflect: To guide a porn struggler, you'll need a clean conscience. You keep your conscience tender if you trust in Christ and resist sin. What's your conscience like? Is it tender, or is it wounded, weak, or hardened?

Act: Ask the Lord to revive your friend's conscience. Pray that he would crack the callous layers and breathe life back into your friend's dead conscience.

13

INSTILLING IDENTITY

A true and enduring identity is a complex gift of
Christ's grace. He gives a new identity in an act of mercy.
Then his Spirit makes it a living reality over a lifetime.
When you see him face to face, you will know him as he truly
is, and you will fully know who you are (1 Cor. 13:12).
—*David Powlison, "Brother, Where Is Your Identity?"*

Therefore, if anyone is in Christ, he is a new creation.
The old has passed away; behold, the new has come.
—*2 Corinthians 5:17*

I (Deepak) asked Sung-woo to tell me about himself. In response, Sung-woo told me about who he is, what he thinks about himself, and the characteristics that define him. These are a few basic aspects of identity. Whenever we speak of identity, we're answering the question "Who am I?"

As a believer, Sung-woo should root his identity firmly in Christ. His truest, deepest, and most fundamental sense of self should be defined by Jesus. But sadly, in Sung-woo's life, as in the lives of the majority of difficult pornography cases, there are identity issues. Sung-woo has functionally lost his sense of identity in Christ because it has been overrun by a life ruled by sexual sin.

Sung-woo was radically converted and became a believer in college. He'd often declare to his friends, "Jesus loves you and me!" His identity struggles started after he finished school. It started with one video when he was twenty-two. He watched a video of people having sex, and, hundreds of videos later, pornography addiction had become a way of life for him. He knew himself to be an addict and couldn't find a way out of the ditch he had created. He felt lost, trapped, and hopeless. His gospel affections died out, and most days his sense of guilt and shame defined him more than any sense of being loved by Christ.

Daniela struggled with porn for three years. She looked at it as a teenager and hid it from most everyone. As her online viewing grew more and more extensive, she became steeped in shame. Doubts nibbled away at her assurance: "How can I be a Christian and keep doing this?" Daniela's lack of assurance was an identity issue because her constant second-guessing undermined her stable sense of being a Christian.

How can we help Daniela and Sung-woo? How can Daniela fight the overwhelming sense that she must *not* be a Christian, as her every act of viewing porn stacks up like evidence that condemns her? What happens to Sung-woo's identity when his carnal desires rule him, his gospel affections have died out, and his sense of the love of Christ is gone?

Our goal in this chapter is to equip you to help Daniela and Sung-woo to fight against the sexual sin that defines their identity and rebuild a stable sense of who they are in Christ. As pastors, disciplers, and caregivers, we must equip strugglers with a proper understanding of their Christian identity. But the question is *how?* As we'll see, a stable Christian identity must be rooted in something outside a struggler, not in the indwelling sin that attempts to redefine him.

ASPECTS OF FUNCTIONAL IDENTITY LOSS

If you ran into Daniela and Sung-woo on a Sunday morning at church and asked them, "Are you Christians?" they'd probably answer yes. Far too many strugglers show up at church with masks on because their shame and guilt make them want to hide their problems. But if you pressed Daniela and Sung-woo, and they were willing to be honest and vulnerable with you, you'd come to find out that *they feel more defined by sin than by Christ*. Sin, not Christ, defines their functional sense of self.

Every time a struggler gives in to the temptation of sexual sin, there is a functional loss of true gospel-centered identity.

- In the moment that he watches a sexually explicit video, Sung-woo believes that the primary purpose of his life is happiness, pleasure, enjoyment, and fulfillment, *not* glorifying God in his body (see 1 Cor. 6:19–20). The godly purposes for his life have been discarded.
- Daniela buys into the false promises that her carnal desires and lusts make to her. She keeps looking at porn because she wants the rewards her sin offers her (see Eph. 4:22; 1 John 2:16). The rewards of her sin come to define her more than the hope of eternal life with God (see Rev. 21:3).
- Tyree lies to himself that his actions have no bearing on anyone else. He doesn't believe that his identity is that of a person who is joined with a larger body of believers, where his sin and suffering impact others (see 1 Cor. 12:12–26). He's foolishly reduced his sense of self to just himself. Like many strugglers, Tyree thinks he can fight his battles on his own.
- Mary-Beth has struggled with pornography and masturbation for so long that her sin has come to define her more than Christ does. Sexual sin has become a way of life for her. Many days, it's taken over her life (see Eph. 4:17–21). She struggles with spiritual amnesia—she's forgotten who she is in Christ because her sin now dominates her life.

Confusion about life's purposes. A life oriented around carnal rewards. An isolated life. Spiritual amnesia. All these symptoms, plus many more, can be found in porn strugglers who have functional identity loss. When their sin defines them more than Christ does, their sin rules their lives. We've looked into the faces of believers who were struggling with pornography and asked, "How much does your sin define you?" "Do you see yourself fundamentally as a porn struggler or as a child of God?" The last time I (Deepak) had this conversation, it was with Sung-woo. Tears streamed down his face as he came to terms with how much his sin had taken over his life as a whole, and especially his identity.

Ask the struggler whom you are discipling, "What defines you more? When you wake up, what do you think about first: the images that you viewed last night or Christ's love for you? When you are walking to work, what defines you more: your sense of shame or your sense of being an adopted child of God?"

Identity confusion arises when a believer's life is oriented around his sin. But identity issues also show up when a believer forgets who God is and what he's done for him. We are far too much like the wilderness generation of Israelites who forgot their deliverance from Egypt. The Lord rescued them from Pharaoh's wrath (see Ex. 5–12) and singlehandedly destroyed the Egyptian army (see Ex. 14:26–28). What did the Israelites do? Whined, complained, and argued with God (see Ex. 16:1–3; 17:2; Ps. 95:10). They forgot about his great acts of redemption and instead got stuck on their petty needs.

As a discipler, you should ask the struggler, "Have you lost sight of God's goodness to you—especially the goodness he has demonstrated so clearly in Christ? Does your functional identity say, 'I'm a porn struggler' and leave out the 'in Christ' part?"

Challenge the struggler's sense of identity that is dominated by sin and a forgetfulness of who God is. Pursue gospel opportunities that will begin the process of reorienting her back to the cross.

GOSPEL RENEWAL FOR DAMAGED IDENTITIES

Let's offer three suggestions for how to renew a struggler's identity through the gospel.

Start with Christ

Our culture communicates that Tyree, Mary-Beth, Daniela, and Sung-woo's identities are rooted in themselves—their thoughts, feelings, and behaviors. *Don't let anyone tell you who you are. Only you have the power to decide your identity.* But basing our identities solely on our thoughts, feelings, or actions leads to problems, Tim Keller explains. "Part of having an identity is having a stable, core sense of who you are, day in and day out, in different settings and times. That is why the traditional way of forging an identity through connection with something solid outside the individual self made sense. But if your identity is just your desires, they are going to be changing all the time."[1] The carnal desires that rule a sexual sinner's life foster an unstable sense of identity. It's rooted in the whims and demands of self-focused and self-glorifying sexual passions. Thus, Keller's sentiments make sense—a stable identity must be found in something outside ourselves.

For the Christian, this stable sense of identity comes in and through Christ. He's the solid rock and firm foundation on which we can stand. The apostle Paul writes in Ephesians 4,

> Now this I say and testify in the Lord, that you must no longer walk as the Gentiles do, in the futility of their minds. They are darkened in their understanding, alienated from the life of God because of the ignorance that is in them, due to their hardness of heart. They have become callous and have given themselves up to sensuality, greedy to practice every kind of impurity. But that is not the way you learned Christ! (vv. 17–20)

Sexual sin confuses a struggler's sense of identity because he believes lies, lives as a slave to his selfish desires, and repeats carnal behaviors, and his heart grows hard and cold. Through all this, his sense of who he is in Christ gets quickly muddled. Slavery to sin and foolishness leads to functional identity loss—who a person is in Christ is a distant memory when sexual sin has overtaken his life and God is forgotten.

Paul exhorts the Ephesians to not forget who they are. "But that is not the way you learned Christ!" (Eph. 4:20). The Ephesians were more than their ethnicity and nationality; they were God's chosen and beloved (see Eph. 1:3–14). The apostle says, "Listen, you're not *primarily* Gentiles anymore!" The Gentiles sounded a lot like porn strugglers—they had "given themselves up to sensuality, greedy to practice every kind of impurity." Paul tells the Ephesian church to stop acting like the Gentiles in the futility of their minds, the darkness of their understanding, their alienation from God, and their ignorance and hardness of heart. "That is not you! That is not the way you learned Christ." Like a loving father, Paul shakes them out of their stupor, calling them to remember who they are in Christ.

It is the same with the people you are helping. Porn strugglers are tempted to forget that they are image bearers of the living God, who calls them to drink from him, not from the empty "cisterns of their own making" (Jer. 2:13 The Voice). Gospel renewal of identity must always start with Christ, the living water. As disciplers, we follow Paul's example—we point strugglers to Christ and beg them to trust in him.

Call for Repentance

Later in the New Testament, Jesus too addresses the church in Ephesus. By this point, it is in danger of losing its way. He warns it, "*Remember* therefore from where you have fallen; repent, and do the works you did at first" (Rev. 2:5).

Another crucial step in renewing a Christian identity is dealing with sin—repenting and doing "the works you did at first." Jesus is speaking to Christians who are wayward. Many of the porn strugglers whom you help are drifting spiritually. Christ calls them to turn from their sins and return to the basics of their faith. He warns them, as he warns us, that if we don't repent, he will come and bring judgment. What a scary thing—to face the judgment of Christ. Be warned.

As a struggling believer faces the reality of judgment, he finds hope by remembering God's grace in Christ. Sexual sin overwhelms his life, so he needs help to see beyond the boundaries of his sin. That's where God's love breaks in—his gospel hope is that repentant sinners can run to Christ. God's love was demonstrated clearly through his Son's death. Tell your struggling friend he must never forget what happened on Calvary. When his fear of judgment and his functional identity loss crash up against gospel hope, point out that he's not alone in the fight.

Offer Regular Gospel Reminders

Because porn strugglers don't know who they are and forget who God is, they must be reminded of who they are in relation to God. This is another way you come into play. Throughout the New Testament,[2] the authors of Scripture exercise the ministry of reminding wayward and suffering believers of important truths. They have given us much to say about the identity of the believer who is battling a pornography addiction. Here is a small and powerful sampling:

- You are complete in Christ (see Col. 2:10).
- You are free from condemnation (see Rom. 8:1).
- You have the righteousness of God through Jesus Christ (see 2 Cor. 5:21).
- You are chosen (see 1 Thess. 1:4).
- You are a partaker of the divine nature (see 2 Peter 1:4).
- You have everlasting life (see John 6:47).
- You can have abundant life (see John 10:10).
- You have access to God by the Holy Spirit (see Eph. 2:18).
- You have Christ in you, the hope of glory (see Col. 1:27).
- You are a new creation (see 2 Cor. 5:17).

A list doesn't change anyone, so much of your role is to exhort the struggler to believe that what God says about him or her is true. Your confidence in God will be contagious. Digging into these truths from Scripture, owning and internalizing them, and living out their reality will change both you and the person you are helping. The psalmist writes,

> How can a young man keep his way pure?
>   By guarding it according to your word.
> With my whole heart I seek you;

> let me not wander from your commandments!
> I have stored up your word in my heart,
>> that I might not sin against you. (Ps. 119:9–11)

As a discipler, you exercise the ministry of gospel reminders. Some days you will sound repetitive: "Remember Christ!" "Trust Christ!" "Don't forget the gospel!" But don't let that deter you. Continue to retell porn strugglers who they are in Christ. We are all forgetful individuals who daily stand in danger of not remembering God's grace, which calls us to live lives of godliness and self-denial.

Praise God for this truth and reality.

Praise God for a gospel identity that is received and not achieved or merited through the struggler's own good works.

Praise God that, through Christ, the believer's personal sense of identity no longer needs to be dominated by sin but is now centered on God's grace.

Reflect: The more confident you are in your own gospel identity, the more of a help you can be as a discipler to a friend who is struggling with pornography. In what ways have your sins or selfish desires hindered your identity in Christ? In what ways does your life need to be reoriented toward Christ?

Act: Together with your friend, work through the Scripture texts on identity in the last section of this chapter and talk through the riches that each verse offers. Be sure to pray that the Holy Spirit applies them to your heart and to the heart of the person you are helping.

PART 2

STRUGGLER SKILLS

Part 1 concentrated on developing the discipler's skills. It's time to switch gears. Part 2 is still written to you as the disicpler, but now you will learn how to help the *struggler* to master skills that he or she needs for the battle against sin.

14

WALKING BY THE SPIRIT

He who dwells in a house, keeps the house in repair;
so the Spirit dwelling in a believer, keeps grace in repair.
—*Thomas Watson,* A Body of Divinity

Nevertheless, I tell you the truth: it is to your advantage that I go
away, for if I do not go away, the Helper will not come to you. But if
I go, I will send him to you.
—*John 16:7*

How does a believer turn away from indwelling sin? Is your friend following the desires of her flesh and the pressures of this world? Or is she being led by the Spirit? The apostle Paul writes, "If we live by the Spirit, let us also keep in step with the Spirit" (Gal. 5:25). Do you, as her discipler, know what this means?

THE PROBLEM: DESIRES OF THE FLESH

Our sinful nature ("the flesh") has its own desires. (We'll look at them in more detail in chapter 16.) For porn strugglers, these desires sound something like this: "I want to escape my stress." "I want to satisfy my bodily urges." "I feel lonely, so I want some intimacy, even if it's from a screen." *I want, I want, I want.* As you come alongside a porn struggler, you'll notice that her sinful nature's carnal desires set the pace for her life. Her fallen desires *drive* what she does. They keep her enslaved to sin and prevent her from doing the things she wants to do (see Gal. 5:17).

There is a war between the desires of the flesh and the desires of the Spirit that's fundamental to any battle with pornography. How does the indwelling Spirit help a struggler to fight a life overrun by the desires of the flesh?

LIVING BY THE SPIRIT

A sinner is redeemed by God, and by faith she is spiritually united to Christ. As she is born again, the Holy Spirit takes up residence in her. We'll find that the Spirit does two things in her life. First, he provides guidance if she's willing to follow him. Second, his strengthening, as well as her union with Christ, gives her power to fight her battles.

Guidance from the Spirit

For any porn struggler, double-mindedness is typical. Janice is stressed out at work, and, in her anxious moments, she feels pulled in two directions. Her carnal desires press her to use porn as an escape; the Spirit tells her to turn to Christ as a refuge. She could give in to the desires that rage within her and scream in her ear, "You've been working so hard. You deserve some pleasure." Or she could listen to the urging of the Spirit: "Trust Christ. He loves you. He'll help you with your stress."

Janice has an opportunity to follow the Spirit's lead. "Walking by the Spirit" pictures people walking in a row or marching in a line. Think of soldiers marching in step, with the sergeant barking out orders. The cadence of the sergeant's orders rings out, and the soldiers' every step is in accordance with his directions. ("Step . . . step . . . step . . . step. . . . Hurry it up! I don't have all day! Step . . . step . . . step . . .") The soldiers stay in line, in their formation, and the only thing they need to do is obey the sergeant's instructions. The NIV appropriately translates Galatians 5:25 as "let us keep *in step* with the Spirit." The Spirit leads, and the only thing we need to do is follow his lead.

The Spirit uses the common means of grace—like Janice's personal devotional life, memorized Scripture verses, fellowship and vital conversations with other believers, regular attendance at church, listening to gospel-centered preaching, and participation the Lord's Supper—to help Janice to reject sin, pursue faithfulness and obedience, and cling to her hope in Christ. The last time she was in a stressful moment at work, Paul's words in Galatians 2:20 came to her mind ("I have been crucified with Christ. It is no longer I who live, but Christ who lives in me"), and the Spirit used the verse to convict Janice to stay the course and not act out by viewing porn. She responded to the Spirit's lead. She prayed, "Lord, this is hard, but with your help I don't have to give in to my desires." It was a small victory, but one that would become more typical in her life with each passing day.

"Since we live by the Spirit, we must also *follow* the Spirit." —Gal. 5:25 HCSB

"Let's keep each step in perfect sync with God's Spirit." —Gal. 5:25 The Voice

Janice doesn't do all this by herself. The apostle Paul is marching in the same formation. Paul says, "Let *us* walk by the Spirit." He includes himself. She is not alone. In fact, in this line is a host of other believers who are fighting the same battle and marching in step with her. Although the devil tries to make her feel alone, Janice is encouraged by the fact that she's in the company of others.

Power from the Spirit

The Spirit also provides strength for Janice's inner being (see Eph. 3:16). There is God-given power available for the porn struggler to fight these battles. She doesn't have to do it by her own strength. Some have described the Holy Spirit as a warrior Spirit. He's here to fight *with* Janice and *in* Janice—to give her what she needs for this battle against porn.

But there is more good news. The apostle Paul tells us that a believer's union with Christ bolsters her ability to put to death the sinful nature's demands and desires. "Those who belong to Christ Jesus have crucified the flesh with its passions and desires" (Gal. 5:24).

We can defeat the sinful nature when we are united to Christ and empowered by the Spirit. It is actually possible. Does the believer you are helping believe that is true? Or has she given in to her sinful nature so often that she's given up hope? Consistent victory over the flesh is possible, and it comes from the Spirit's power. This is the apostle Paul's promise: "Walk by the Spirit, and you *will not* gratify the desires of the flesh" (Gal. 5:16).

Putting sin to death and following the lead of the Spirit go hand in hand. They are not two separate things; rather, they are two sides of the same coin. But one drives the other. As Janice lives according to the Spirit's direction and strength, God gives her the power to put to death the sinful desires of her flesh.

HELPING THE STRUGGLER TO WALK BY THE SPIRIT

Who is setting the agenda for your friend's life—is it his sinful flesh, or is it the Spirit? Be honest. What do you really think?

Here's what we'd like you to do—ask your friend a range of questions that might bring the truth to light:

- When you wake up in the morning, how self-reliant are you?
- Do you walk into the day with your game plan, your desires, your dreams, your goals, your expectations, and your schemes charting the course? Or do you turn to God and say, "Lord God, I need your help"; "Holy Spirit, come, lead the way"; "I can't do this on my own—only you can"?
- When was the last time phrases like the ones above came out of your mouth? Have you recently pleaded for the Spirit to direct your life?

Don't wait any longer. Persuade your friend to give up his own schemes to access pornography and instead to follow the Spirit's lead in his life. He can't defeat this problem through his own power but only through the Holy Spirit's strength.

Reflect: What goals, dreams, hopes, and agendas does your friend need to give up right now in order to let the Spirit take control of her life? Janice was driven by her achievement-oriented goals at work, which caused her to ignore many of the common means of grace, like Bible intake, prayer, and regular attendance at church. She came to realize that her desires for success were grounded not in God's glory but in her own and that this was impeding the work of the Spirit in her life. She committed to the Lord that she would work for him and no longer for herself.

Act: Don't let another moment pass without turning to God and asking for the Spirit's help. Pray now, with humility, begging God to set the agenda for your friend's life. If you commit to following the Spirit's lead, that will set a good example for your friend, and, ultimately, it will be what's best for your own soul too.

15

OVERCOMING TEMPTATIONS

No one ever regretted saying no *to temptations.*
—Ed Welch, *"How to Slay the Dragon of Pornography"*

Watch and pray that you may not enter into temptation. The spirit indeed is willing, but the flesh is weak.
—Matthew 26:41

Ava stared at the book. The cover displayed a muscular man embracing a beautiful woman; they were deep in a kiss and mostly unclothed. She felt the allure. For several years Ava had read erotic novels, partly for the romance but mostly for the steamy sex scenes. The graphic descriptions of sex captivated her imagination and stirred her yearnings from within. But she walked away after each book feeling guilty and ashamed. As she held the book in her hands, the justifications came knocking at her door: "God's hasn't given you a husband, so you deserve this." "Just one more, and then you'll stop." "All your friends are doing it, so why not you too?"

Oliver held the cell phone in his hands. It was an old one, and, until ten minutes ago, he hadn't realized it was still around. His current phone was locked down—no browser, no access to the app store, no shortcuts to illicit pictures. He couldn't get to anything explicit. But this old phone would give him unfettered access to the forbidden. He felt the force of the temptation. His sinful nature was muttering, "Indulge a little before you tell your accountability partner."

Ava and Oliver wanted to resist. They desperately wanted to fight. But they felt helpless as temptation whispered sweet promises.

Temptations are daily battles, common to all. But how and when to fight temptation is, at times, perplexing to Christians. What does battling temptation look like? What helps a believer to fight back and not get entangled? What gives hope in the face of Satan's schemes?

And what is temptation in the first place?

WHAT IS TEMPTATION?

In its essence, temptation is when evil beckons a believer to turn away from God (see Prov. 7:10–20). This evil may come from outside or inside the believer, and, in the words of John Owen, it "exerts a force" and "seduces" a believer's heart. It tests a believer's ability to resist sin and stay obedient to God.

"Temptation . . . in *general*, is any thing, state, way, or condition that, upon any account whatsoever, has a force or efficacy to seduce, to draw the mind and heart of a man from its obedience, which God requires of him, into any sin, in any degree of it whatsoever.

"In *particular*, that is a temptation to any man which causes . . . him to sin, or in anything to go off from his duty, either by bringing evil into his heart, or drawing out that evil that is in his heart, or any other way diverting him from communion with God and that constant, equal, universal obedience . . . that is required of him.

". . . Be it what it will, that from anything whatsoever, within us or without us, has advantage to hinder in duty, or to provoke unto or in any way to occasion for sin—that is a temptation, and so to be looked on. . . . That soul lies at the brink of ruin who discerns it not." —**John Owen**[1]

Temptations from both outside (see Prov. 5:3–6, 20; 7:10–27) and inside (see Prov. 6:25) the believer threaten to destroy him. On the outside, Satan prowls around like a lion looking for victims to consume (see 1 Peter 5:8–9). Satan lies to them as he tempts them to disobey God and go elsewhere to find satisfaction and joy (see

Ps. 16:11). On the inside, a believer's carnal desires lure and entice him to sin (see James 1:13–17). Like an animal attracted to bait, the believer falters in the face of inner and outer temptations. His fleshly desires are at war with the Spirit's desires (see Gal. 5:16–17), and there are moments when the believer feels like he is losing. Although the situation seems desperate, the story of temptation is a hopeful one for believers, as we will see, because our hope of fighting temptations is in and through Christ.

A SHORT HISTORY OF TEMPTATIONS

God knows us, and, as our Creator, he determines what is good for us. From the very beginning, he set up boundaries for us. If we live *within* his boundaries, we live according to the purposes he has set out for us. To live *without* his boundaries is to disregard God and say he doesn't know what he's doing. Temptations entice us to traverse God's boundaries to get what we want and to ignore what God intends for our good.

In the garden of Eden, God created boundaries for Adam and Eve. He said to the first couple, "You can partake in the fruit of any tree, just not *this one*" (see Gen. 2:16–17). Temptation immediately followed. Adam and Eve were tempted from without as Satan planted seeds of doubt ("Did God actually say . . . ?"—Gen. 3:1) and outright lied to them ("You will not surely die"—Gen. 3:4). There was also a temptation from within: Adam and Eve desired the forbidden fruit. When we listen to Satan, follow our desires, ignore God's boundaries, and no longer live as God intends, we become less than fully human.[2]

Every generation that has followed Adam and Eve has faced temptations. The history of the Old Testament is one of Israel's being tested. As the Israelites experienced challenging circumstances, they showed they would not be content with what God had given them. They rejected manna and longed for more extravagant foods from Egypt (see Num. 11), they rejected leaders like Moses (see Num. 12; 14), and so much more. The first generation failed and wandered in the desert for forty years, and later generations failed and were thrown into exile. Israel's failings were recorded as lessons for our good (see 1 Cor. 10:1–11), because we too are tempted.

The essence of all temptation—for Adam and Eve, for Israel, and also for us—comes down to the question of who or what the believer will worship in the moment. Will she be a slave to her sin, or will she trust in God, the giver of all good gifts (see James 1:17)? Will she believe the essential, core message of temptation: *There is something better out there for you than what God has given you?* Adam, Eve, and Israel bought into this lie. Will your struggling friend do the same?

Atheism is at the core of all sexual sin—a lack of belief that God intends good for us and a carnal desire to find satisfaction elsewhere. The threefold alliance that we all face—the world, our flesh, and Satan—conspire together to peddle this message.

Make no mistake: Satan is after a struggling believer. (We'll outline more of his schemes in the next section.) Your friend can resist the devil, and he will flee (see James 4:7). She can fight with the armor that God provides—truth, faith, righteousness, the Word, and the Spirit (see Eph. 6:10–20). But we can't reduce this fight to the believer's ability to resist temptation. In the ongoing war against temptation, God's ultimate provision comes through Christ. With God's strength, a struggling believer can overcome. God will not allow her to be tempted beyond her ability to resist; he will provide a way out (see 1 Cor. 10:13). God's grace is greater than the devil's power to tempt. The Lord can help the struggler to resist temptation and say no. But the struggling believer is not perfect; only Christ is. Realistically, there are days when she will fail. God's forgiveness in Christ gives her hope to continue. The Lord patiently waits for her, picking her up off the ground and helping her to face a new day and continue the fight.

Jesus entered into our world, faced temptation, and emerged with a perfect record, without ever having failed. Christ, led by the Spirit, went into the desert to face Satan—who tempted our Lord with control, hunger, significance, and power (see Matt. 4:1–11). Jesus is not like us. We fail in the face of temptation. Christ overcame. His righteousness was demonstrated through his defying of the devil's temptations. His perfect obedience and full resistance to evil set him apart and prepared him to be the perfect Savior. Jesus gets what we're going through. He's not distant and removed from us. He was tempted in every respect, just as we are, and yet never sinned (see Heb. 4:15). Because he was tempted, he is able to sympathize with our weakness. What a wonderful Savior!

SATAN'S DEVICES, BAITS, AND TRAPS

Before we teach you how to fight temptation through Christ, we'll take one last step. To be a good discipler, you must be able to recognize and point out Satan's typical schemes. Satan's goal is to destroy Christians. He uses bait and traps to lure them into sin. His methods are predictable and can be discerned from both Scripture and life experience. Let's take a look at how this plays out for the porn struggler.

A Seductive Approach

The Proverbial adulteress doesn't passively wait. She comes out and finds men who lack sense (see Prov. 7:7, 15). She uses her persuasive words and body to lure youth to their spiritual deaths (see Prov. 5:3–6, 20). "So now I have come out to meet you, to seek you eagerly. . . . I have spread my couch with coverings. . . . Come, let us take our fill of love till morning . . . for my husband is not at home" (Prov. 7:15–16, 18–19). She begs and pleads with her target, insistently luring him until he finally gives in.

In the same way, the devil uses the lure of sex and beautiful bodies to entice a believer to sin. Think about the world we live in. It's very common to see immodestly dressed men and women in movies, advertisements, and magazines and on television, billboards, and social media—as well as walking down the street. I (Deepak) was walking through a local college campus at the start of the spring. I was dismayed by how much skin was exposed by the students around me. A sexualized culture daily tempts us with messages like "Have sex! Take what you want and feel no shame." And, just like the adulteress of Proverbs, the devil suggests that sexual sin will be enjoyable and free of consequences.

An Incremental Approach

Ralph thinks he'll indulge in just one sin. The whispers of Satan sound like this: "Just one more. One more R-rated sex scene. One more carnal thought. One more lustful look at a coworker. One more explicit picture or video. One more time masturbating. One more time taking off clothes or rubbing against another person. Just one more." But Satan doesn't want Ralph to stop with one sin. His goal is to seduce and persuade Ralph to keep going. The devil wants Ralph's life to be ruined by sexual sin. "Nothing bad will come of this. No one will be hurt by this. So enjoy yourself!" Does this approach sound familiar?

A Subtle and Subversive Approach

Satan knows that he would not be nearly as successful if he bluntly demanded, "Hey, you should look at a naked woman today." No . . . temptation is much more subtle and subversive. Kai has three weeks of reprieve from porn. He thinks, "I'm doing okay. Looks like I can handle this now." With that little thought, pride slips in the side door, and Kai becomes more vulnerable to porn. It is no surprise that he falls again the next week.

The Bait and Hook Approach

Temptation *looks* good, but its end is anything but. Satan persuaded Eve when he whispered, "I have something better to offer you than God does!" His offer looked good—Adam's and Eve's eyes would be opened, and they would be like God (see Gen. 3:5). The devil offered bait with a hidden hook—a golden cup of sweet liquid that turned out to be poison.[3] Adam and Eve took the fruit, tasted the poison, and ended up in exile from the garden, suffering, and eventually dead.

The devil offers your friend the bait without showing him the hook. The Evil One ensnares and ambushes rather than launching a full frontal attack.

- Julianna clicks on a gym advertisement that promises a healthier and more fit life (the bait). It reveals muscular bodies with tight clothing (the hook), and she starts to get aroused.

- Carlos is on social media and notices a picture of an old high-school girlfriend (the bait). He clicks on her account and scrolls through it, stumbling across pictures of her in a bikini (the hook). The sight makes him long for intimacy with her again.
- Cheryl goes on a camping trip with a group of friends from church (the bait). On the trip, some people in the group jump in the river for a swim. Many of the guys strip off their shirts, and Cheryl is mesmerized by several of the more athletic men (the hook). Filled with lust, she can't take her eyes off them.

False Appearances and Diminishing Returns

In C. S. Lewis's *Screwtape Letters*, the demons Wormwood and Screwtape have a conversation about how sin must be packaged in order to sell it to believers:

> Never forget that when we are dealing with any pleasure in its healthy and normal and satisfying form, we are, in a sense, on the [Lord's] ground. I know we have won many a soul through pleasure. All the same, it is His invention, not ours. He made the pleasures: all our research so far has not enabled us to produce one. All we can do is to encourage the humans to take the pleasures which [the Lord] has produced, at times, or in ways, or in degrees, which He has forbidden. Hence we always try to work away from the natural condition of any pleasure to that in which it is least natural, least redolent of its Maker, and least pleasurable. An ever increasing craving for an ever diminishing pleasure is the formula.[4]

The devil knows. God's pleasures are good, but, when distorted and amplified, they can overrun a life. When a believer's carnal desires get out of hand, the thrill of pornography becomes less exhilarating with every session. That leaves a struggler longing for more and never satisfied.

HOW BELIEVERS FIGHT TEMPTATION

If we know this is the battle plan of the Enemy, how can we equip others to withstand temptation? Here are a few practices to put in a Christian's arsenal of defense.

Watch and Pray

Jesus arrived at the garden of Gethsemane and, leaving his disciples behind, gave them just one command: "Watch with me" (Matt. 26:38). He went away, prayed to the Father, and returned to find his disciples asleep. Jesus turned to Peter and said, "Could you not watch with me one hour? Watch and pray that you may not enter into temptation" (Matt. 26:40–41). When we are fighting temptation, we must follow Jesus's command to watch and pray. What does that mean for us and for our struggling friends?

Watch. Watchfulness is a constant state of alertness and vigilance against temptation. It's similar to the military's idea of maintaining situational awareness—"a proactive posture whereby [a person] pays active attention to themselves and their surroundings."[5]

The Puritan John Owen, in his classic work on temptation, expands on this idea of being watchful and vigilant in the face of temptation.

- We should stay alert and vigilant so that we can detect temptation early rather than waiting until we are entangled and overwhelmed by it.[6]
- We should fear temptation, recognizing its dangers. If we consider temptation a light or trivial matter, we'll get trapped by it. If we enter into temptation with great caution, we'll be prepared to do battle with it.[7]
- We should be especially wary of the dangers that come with particular seasons of life—for example, times of prosperity, spiritual dryness, or great success.[8]
- We should be watchful of our own hearts, being fully aware of the ways in which we're wired—our temperaments, our

natural propensities, our personalities. We should also pay careful attention to our sinful patterns and weaknesses.[9]
- We should be alert to the occasions or situations in which our natural propensities typically lead us to sin.[10] Whatever these occasions, we should stay far away from them.

Pray. In the garden of Gethsemane, Jesus also asked his friends to pray in the face of temptation. Again, Owen has several suggestions about what this means for all believers.

- Because Jesus asked the Father to keep us, we should pray the same thing for others. Our Savior prayed, "My prayer is not that you take them out of the world but that you protect them from the evil one" (John 17:15 NIV). So also we pray for God to shield, guard, and keep our friends in the face of temptation.[11]
- We should pray for the Lord's provision and strength for our friends. *We* cannot save them when they are in the midst of temptation.[12] Rather, they need the Lord's help to overcome. When the apostle tells us to fight the devil's schemes and put on the armor of God, he also says we should pray "at all times in the Spirit, with all prayer and supplication" and "keep alert with all perseverance, making supplication for all the saints" (Eph. 6:18). Our friends should put on the Lord's armor, but, at the same time, they need God's sustaining power.
- We must pray always (see Luke 18:1).[13] Believers who are in constant prayer will be much more ready when temptation comes than those who are prayerless.

Make Ample Gospel Provisions before Temptation Strikes

The psalmist writes, "I have stored up your word in my heart, that I might not sin against you" (Ps. 119:11), and Jesus says, "The good person out of the good treasure of his heart produces good" (Luke 6:45). By consistently reading, understanding, and applying God's Word, a believer stores up good in her heart and trusts the

Lord to produce good in her life. God's Word will also preserve and protect her from the dangers of sexual sin (see Prov. 6:20, 23–24).

"Our hearts, as our Savior speaks, are our treasury. There we lay up whatsoever we have, good or bad; and thence do we draw it for our use (Matt. 12:35). It is the heart, then, wherein provision is to be laid up against temptation. When an enemy draws night to a fort or castle to besiege and take it, oftentimes, if he find it well manned and furnished with provision for a siege, and so able to hold out, he withdraws and assaults it not. If Satan, the prince of this world, come and find our hearts fortified against his batteries, and provided to hold out, he not only departs, but, as James says, he flees: 'He will flee from us' (4:7). For the provision to be laid up it is that which is provided in the gospel for us. Gospel provisions will do this work; that is, keep the heart full of a sense of the love of God in Christ. This is the greatest preservative against the power of temptation in the world." —**John Owen**[14]

God's Word, and especially the good news of the gospel, is crucial to a believer's battle. The gospel is the good news that Jesus died and rose again for sinners. The gospel is not an *intellectual* idea to be acknowledged and accepted; rather, it's the news about Jesus as a *personal* Savior. Christ himself is the struggler's hope, strength, and provision against temptations.

All the common means of grace—personal study of God's Word, prayer, fellowship with believers, regular attendance at church, expositional preaching, participation in the Lord's Supper—build up the gospel storehouse of provisions in a believer's heart. A struggler shouldn't wait for temptation to strike before gathering up God's Word in his heart and gathering with God's people. Rather, he should gather up gospel provisions for his heart (a trust in Christ, a cherishing of the gospel, and all the common means of grace) so that his soul becomes well defended against the baits and traps of the devil.[15]

The greater a believer's confidence in Christ's love for her, the better prepared she is for any temptation that the devil throws at her. The more she doubts Christ's love, the more she should fear, for she has very little stored up to help her to fight. Why wait? She must run to Christ. Encourage her to do everything she can to grow in her confidence of God's love in Christ and to bask in its security and safety.[16]

Keep a Log of Your Encounters with Temptations

Satan's battle plan is not hidden. We see from Scripture (see Job 1–3; Eph. 6:10–20; 1 Peter 5:8–9) and learn from experience how the devil exploits our weaknesses. With all this knowledge to help us, we would be foolish to not recognize temptation to sin when it appears.

Ask your struggling friend to keep a log of her difficulties with temptation.[17] You can lay the foundation for the log by asking some general questions about the nature of the temptation she experiences.

- Where are you, and what are you typically doing, when temptation comes on?
- When temptation last struck, were you alert and vigilant or unprepared and lazy? Did temptation catch you off guard?
- How can you be better prepared the next time temptation comes?
- What triggers you toward temptation? What baits and traps does the devil like to use on you?
- If you resisted the temptation, how did you do it?[18]
- What lies or inaccurate pictures of God are your temptations communicating to you?
- What promises of God are you tempted to forget in the heat of temptation?
- What amplifies the voice of temptation in your life?
- Do you pray? What do you pray when you are tempted?
- Which of your sin patterns and weaknesses are most commonly exposed by temptation? Were any of them exposed the last time you were tempted?
- Did anything else correlate with the sexual temptations?[19]

Ask your friend to take some time to write this out and think through her engagement with temptation. Greater self-awareness helps believers to be better prepared the next time temptation comes knocking at their door.

Trust in a Perfect Savior

We can fight temptations because of Christ. He's worthy of our trust.

He never failed.

He was perfectly obedient.

He never turned away from the Father.

He never got entangled by sin. He headed it off early on.

He used the Word to speak back to the devil.

He could not be seduced by evil words.

He understands our temptations in every respect.

He sympathizes with us because he gets it.

Struggling believers cower and falter in the face of temptation. But not Christ. C. S. Lewis explains, "Only those who try to resist temptation know how strong it is. . . . We never find out the strength of the evil impulse inside us until we try to fight it: and Christ, because He was the only man who never yielded to temptation, is also the only man who knows to the full what temptation means—the only complete realist."[20] Your struggling friend may give in to temptation before it is fully spent, but only Christ overcame and resisted the full force of temptation.[21] Jesus lived a perfect life by submitting his whole heart—both body and soul—at every moment to the obedience of his Father God. Imagine that! Imagine if, instead of having sexual sin as its foregone conclusion, sexual temptation was a means by which we were molded into the image of Jesus Christ!

We often find in believers a *fait accompli* mentality when it comes to sexual temptation. It's as if they've already lost the battle in their minds, long before temptation strikes. This does not have to be so. We can act in faith, trusting in God's promise that he will preserve the believer during temptation.[22] We can meet temptation when it first appears with a wholehearted trust in the Savior. Why? Because we know Christ cares: "Because he himself has suffered when tempted, he is able to help those who are being tempted" (Heb. 2:18).

How does trusting Jesus help us? What does his help look like? God provides strength—supernatural power—for the battle. He helps us to be vigilant, make wise choices, and run when temptation strikes. But more than just providing strength, trusting in Christ gives us someone to depend on aside from ourselves. We often see strugglers lose the battle of temptation when they rely solely on themselves. As disciplers, we can't win this battle for our friends, but we can encourage them to depend on the One who can.

Reflect: Think about your own battles with temptation. What has God taught you, and how can you use that wisdom to help your struggling friend?

Act: In your next conversation, use the questions from the temptation log to better understand the struggler's battle.

Act: One way to fight temptation is to train strugglers to notice early warning signs and bring their difficulties to the light long before they sin. Consider a river.

> *Upstream* are the struggler's early warning signs—a *sexually explicit thought*; maybe a *difficult emotion*, such as despair over his singleness, self-pity, anger over a missed promotion at work, frustration with his wife over lack of intimacy in their marriage, hurt following a perceived rejection from his boss, or the sense that he is a third wheel with his married friends; *an unexpected exposure* to something tantalizing, such as a scantily clad woman walking by or a swimsuit or underwear ad on the sidebar of a website.
>
> When the struggler is upstream, he has to *pay attention to his triggers*. If he notices the triggers early, he can take

active steps to flee the temptation. If he is passive about the triggers, the natural downstream flow of the river will keep him moving toward acting out. There are *obvious* triggers, like a woman in revealing clothing, and *less obvious* ones, like a moment of frustration at his wife. Both kinds of triggers matter.[23]

Midstream is *fantasizing* (drawing up images in his mind and turning them into a full-blown movie reel), *scheming* (making plans to watch an explicit movie and masturbate after he gets home), or *making preparations* (stopping by the library to pick up a sexually explicit novella or movie).

Downstream is where the struggler commits sexual sin— viewing explicit images or videos, sexting, masturbating, reading a sex-riddled novel, or writing out a sexualized piece of fan fiction to arouse himself.

The tendency of a sexual struggler is to confess sin *after* he's been downstream. He doesn't bring light to the situation or let his accountability know about his struggles early on. But imagine if he texted two close friends the moment he had a few sexually explicit thoughts and said, "I'm struggling right now in my mind. Can you pray for me and then call to check on me tonight?" That quick confession exposes the struggle and catches it early in the battle against temptation.

This won't come easily. The sinful nature makes the river naturally flow downstream. The momentum of the river is always heading in the direction of committing sexual sin. To help a believer, you need to persuade and train him to expose his temptations early. The earlier the better.

16

KILLING OR REPLACING BAD DESIRES

Be killing sin or it will be killing you.
—*John Owen*, On the Mortification of Sin

Now the serpent was more crafty than any other beast of the field that the Lord God had made. He said to the woman, "Did God actually say, 'You shall not eat of any tree in the garden'?"
—*Genesis 3:1*

Isabella stares at the screen. She's been writing a steamy sex scene for a popular fan fiction website. She can't and won't look at explicit naked photos or watch videos of people having sex. She went through a brief stage of doing that, and her guilt and shame were overwhelming. Writing erotic fan fiction is another way for her to feed her desires for the illicit and use her creative energy. She knows she shouldn't do it, but she rationalizes it away. "It's just creative writing." "No one is hurt by this." Her yearning to satisfy her lustful cravings is strong.

Mason is poking around his smartphone when he realizes that his favorite sports app takes him to YouTube whenever it links to a video. He blocked YouTube on his phone a long time ago and restricted the app store so he couldn't download anything. Yet the moment he discovers a back door to watching videos, he takes the plunge without even thinking. He types in the words *naked women*, and illicit videos pop up. Thirty minutes later, he is still watching. His desires for porn are strong, and they keep getting stronger each minute he views sexually explicit videos.

What's a desire? Scripture uses the word to describe our wants (see 1 Tim. 2:8; James 1:14–15; 4:2; 2 Peter 1:4; 3:3; Jude 1:7)—our strong yearnings to have something. For Christians, the desires of our hearts are a natural outworking of either our sinful nature ("our flesh") or our redeemed nature, and they motivate and orient our lives. The desires of our flesh motivate us to do the things we should not do or not do the things we should do. The desires of our redeemed nature arise from the grace of God and the work of the indwelling Spirit, and they motivate us to love Christ and obey him.

Every believer has a mixture of sinful (bad) and redeemed (good) desires that are at war with each other in his or her heart (see Luke 6:43–45; Gal. 5:17–24; James 1:14–15). Isabella and Mason have sinful desires that give rise to using pornography and writing sexually explicit fiction. The expression of their lusts is different, but the basic DNA of their desires is the same.

How can we help a struggling believer to kill or replace bad desires? That's what we'll cover in this chapter.

GOOD AND BAD SEXUAL DESIRES

We understand from Scripture that sexual desires—physical, emotional, and spiritual cravings for intimacy with the opposite sex—are a good thing. They are a gift of God. It's a kindness of the Lord to give us such delight in our spouses and to allow two people to lovingly and mutually give pleasure to and receive it from each other. Sex is a spiritual act, not merely a physical one, when it takes place in the context of a covenant union between a husband and wife. It's done to the glory of God when love, trust, and safety under-gird the marriage. Good sexual desires for intimacy with a spouse are woven into the fabric of who we are as image bearers.

If there are good desires for sexual intimacy, then *lusts* are desires for sexual intimacy that have gone bad. They go against biblical boundaries and God's good design for sex in marriage. They become much more selfish in nature. And they exploit and dehumanize fellow image bearers. The biblical authors most often use the term *lust* the context of warnings against inappropriate sex or sexual immorality (see Ezek. 23:5–20; Matt. 5:28; Rom. 1:24; 1 Thess. 4:5; 2 Peter 2:10). Lusts are passions for what God has forbidden.

In that same sense, John Freeman defines lust as "that heart-hunger in me that denies and disavows those made in the image of God, whether it's another man or another woman, and reduces them to what I can get out of them to feed (and fill) my hungry heart right now. This means that by nature, our lusts twist, devour, consume, and use others for our own benefit."[1] This definition helpfully speaks not only to our sexual cravings ("I want you") but also to how we use and exploit other image bearers to satisfy our carnal desires.

Lusts are disordered desires. They are good desires gone bad. They are the epitome of selfishness and self-centeredness, especially because they lead people to take advantage of other image bearers to satisfy their self-centered urges and wants.

An addict's heart is corrupted and his perspective on sex is distorted by porn. It's common for a porn addict to confuse lustful desires with God-given cravings for sexual intimacy. But how does that happen? How do good desires morph into something bad?

WHEN GOOD DESIRES TURN BAD

Contrary to common belief, as image bearers we can't be reduced to our sexual desires. Sexual longing is just one of many rich desires that God has instilled within us. Consider a few examples of good desires that can turn bad.

The Good	The Bad
I will be diligent and thoughtful about my work because I want to be a good steward of the job God has given me.	I'm too eager for success. I desire to be more than just average. I'll probably turn into a workaholic because I must achieve and be the best at what I do.

I desire to give away money and possessions to the poor because it's godly to take care of fellow image bearers who need help.	I want more money. Money has become my god.
I want to become a preacher of God's Word because I'm excited to see how it will change lives.	I want to be in the pulpit because I seek more attention. It makes me feel better about myself.
I desire to be intimate with my spouse because it's an important way to build unity in our marriage.	I crave sexual intimacy. I will manipulate and use my spouse to have more sex so I can satisfy my lusts and because I feel entitled to sex in marriage.
I desire sexual intimacy with a spouse because the Bible says it's a good thing and because I want the closeness that intimacy affords.	My life will not be complete without marriage and sex. I desire a spouse and sexual intimacy because I feel like I must satisfy my bodily urges and I don't like being lonely.

How does a good desire turn bad? How does a person move from a good longing to a selfish one? Sin takes a good desire, and, like an oil spill in a clear blue ocean, *sin contaminates and spoils it.* Sin messes it up. It takes a desire that's godly or wise and makes it selfish. A young man or woman goes from desiring a godly spouse (a longing the Bible commends—see Prov. 12:4; 18:22; 31:10) and desiring intimacy with a spouse (see Prov. 5:18–19) to lusting after pictures of naked people he or she doesn't know.

But what's the movement from good to bad? How do we get from one to the other?

Ungodly Responses to a Fallen World

Good desires turn bad when a believer responds sinfully to the difficulties and pressures of her life. Brenda, a single woman, wants to get married. But she has no marriage prospects, hasn't dated anyone in five years, and is now in her late thirties. She desires a godly spouse and intimacy with a husband. If not relieved, her *distress* ("Will I be lonely for the rest of my life?") moves to a *demand* ("God, you must give me a spouse. I can't live alone for the rest of my life"). If not relieved, her *demand* turns into *disregard* ("God, if you don't give me a spouse, then I no longer trust in your care for me. I'm going to go at it my own way and ditch your ways"). Underneath Brenda's disregard is unbelief and lack of trust in God's character.

Adoption of Ungodly Motives

Under the pressure of her difficult circumstances, Brenda's motives change. When she started out as a Christian, she desired marriage and intimacy with a spouse because the Bible commends it, she personally hoped for it, and she wanted to have children. But the longer she stays single, the more she adopts ungodly motivations ("I must satisfy my bodily urges"; "I hate loneliness"; "I must have control of my life since God won't give me what I want").

Transformation of Our Desires

As Brenda faces the difficulties of her fallen world, her heart responds sinfully (with distress, demand, disregard) and she adopts ungodly motives. Her good desires change and become *inordinate*—taking on greater weight and importance than they deserve. Like a man who never exercises, eats too much fatty food, and quickly grows overweight, an inordinate desire grows to be disproportionate.

Brenda desires a husband and intimacy in marriage. God denies this to her and makes her wait. The longer she goes without marriage and intimacy, the older she gets and the more she longs for a spouse and marriage. The cry of her heart is "Lord, don't you love me? Why won't you give it to me? How long, O Lord, must I wait?" Her selfish heart assigns more and more importance to her good desires for a spouse and intimacy, out of proportion to what is appropriate.

The Lord uses his Word, his people, and the indwelling Spirit to help his people to moderate their desires and keep them at an appropriate level of importance. But as her prospects of marriage dwindle,

Brenda chooses to respond sinfully to her extended singleness. Her good and godly desires for marriage and intimacy take on idolatrous proportions in her heart.

An inordinate desire, if thought about, talked about, sought after, and cultivated, can ascend to the place of a *ruling desire*—a craving that's overtaken a believer's life. This happens as Brenda reorients her life, her thoughts, and her goals to get this desire ("I must have sexual experiences"). Her desire has ascended to the throne of her heart and has (in reality) even displaced Christ.

Brenda's ruling desire leads to bad fruit as she pursues porn and masturbation to satisfy her desire. She thinks, "Since God doesn't care and I can't have intimacy with a spouse right now, I will look at porn and masturbate to feed my desire for sexual experiences."

THE NATURE OF BAD DESIRES

Now that we know how good desires turn bad, we need to understand two things about bad desires. Bad desires are *insatiable* and *warlike*.

Bad Desires Are Never Satisfied

Picture your friend as a valiant knight. Across from him is an enormous fire-breathing dragon. It stares at your friend. Drool drips from its mouth. This dragon is your friend's sinful nature. It's his flesh.

We've seen that Scripture teaches us that the sinful nature ("the flesh") has its own desires (see Gal. 5:17). It has cravings, wants, and longings. Sin contaminates our good desires and turns them bad, and the flesh eggs us on: "Look at another naked image." "Don't trust God." "Give in to your sin—you deserve it." "Enjoy your lust." "You need more sexual satisfaction."

The apostle Paul warns us to not make provisions for our flesh (see Rom. 13:14), but whenever your friend looks at pornography, he is feeding this beast. When he looks at naked pictures or watches explicit videos, he's throwing the dragon a juicy steak to sustain it. He's feeding his flesh's desires. The more he gives it, the more it grows. And it always wants more. It's *never* content and fulfilled. The only way to destroy this beast's power is to starve it and put it to death.

Bad Desires Are Warlike

The desires of our sinful nature are at war with our redeemed nature. The stark reality of this battle is that if your friend doesn't kill the desires of his flesh, they will ruin his life. The dragon lunges at him. He holds up his shield and swings his sword with all his strength. He fights; it attacks. He protects himself and then goes on the offensive. The dragon steps back, but only temporarily. They are both constantly battling each another.

The apostle Paul writes, "The desires of the flesh are against the Spirit, and the desires of the Spirit are against the flesh, for these are opposed to each other, to keep you from doing the things you want to do" (Gal. 5:17). The Spirit in the believer is in hand-to-hand combat with the believer's flesh because the Spirit and the flesh want different things. Their war is a daily reality for every believer. On the days that the flesh is winning, it keeps your friend from doing what he wants to do. Some days Christians are victorious; other days we lose the struggle against the flesh.

HOW WE GET RID OF BAD DESIRES AND RETURN TO GOOD DESIRES

Here are the million-dollar questions: What do we do to get these selfish, carnal desires out of our struggling friends' lives? How do we eliminate them? How do they change? How do we revive our friends' good desires for Christ and healthy sexual intimacy?

A believer who is struggling with pornography use is confused about good and bad desires. His addiction to pornography has blurred his perspective on what is a pornified desire and what is a God-honoring and healthy sexual desire. Matt Fradd explains, "A desire for sex is a sign of health. A desire for porn is not. One reason many people find it difficult to break free from porn and remain free is that they confuse sexual desire with a craving for pornography. . . . The goal is not the long-term squelching of sexual desire. The goal is the healing of your sexual cravings so that you pursue them in a manner that pushes you toward a healthy and satisfying marital relationship."[2] Our process of change is for us to grow in self-awareness of bad desires, starve and then kill the unhealthy pornified desires, and revive our long-gone gospel affections. But to stop here is to fall short. Like Matt Fradd said, we don't want to squelch good sexual desire. We want to revive healthy desires for sexual intimacy.

In such an oversexualized culture, how do we identify good and healthy sexual desires? What's most healthy for us is to live according to God's good design for sexuality. God's Word traces out the boundaries for sexual intimacy (marriage with one spouse of the opposite sex). As we treasure the One who is the giver of every good gift (see James 1:17), we also learn to cherish the boundaries he sets up for our lives.

Discover Their Desires

John Freeman points out that not everyone is self-aware enough to know what desires are at war in his own heart. Before a person repents, he needs to know what he's supposed to repent of! Solomon writes, "The purpose in a man's heart is like deep water, but a man of understanding will draw it out" (Prov. 20:5). Just as we lower a bucket into a deep well to draw out the water at the bottom, we must probe into the hearts of sinners and draw out what motivates and calibrates them. One way for us to do this is to ask thoughtful questions that draw out strugglers' deeper motives and help them to become more self-aware of their own hearts. It takes love and patience to use careful, heart-oriented questions to unearth the muck that resides in a struggler's heart.[3] (If you're not sure how to do this, review chapter 6 on asking the right questions.)

Starve Their Inordinate Desires

What if you took the dragon and put him on a diet for a year? What if you starved him—no food and water for six months?

Scripture commands us to "abstain from the passions of the flesh, which wage war against your soul" (1 Peter 2:11). The biblical authors consistently warn us against participating in sexual immorality (see Acts 15:20; Rom. 13:13; 1 Cor. 10:8) and commend a lifestyle of purity in which believers deny the carnal desires of the flesh (see 2 Cor. 6:6; 1 Tim. 4:12; 5:2).

Here's our strategy: We help strugglers to actively starve their flesh of its access to pornography. The longer we starve it, the more likely it is that this beast will die. The strong hold that the sinful flesh has on a struggling believer's life, the power that the beast wields in his heart and mind, can be weakened—and, with time, it can be broken.

First Peter 2:11 ("abstain from the passions of the flesh") and Romans 13:14 ("make no provision for the flesh") show us that we must starve these desires. We don't starve them simply to make the flesh slimmer, like people on a radical diet. Our goal is to starve the flesh so that its lustful desires die. In Galatians 5:24, Paul tells us that "those who belong to Christ Jesus have crucified the flesh with its passions and desires" (see also Rom. 6:6). Our ultimate objective is to slaughter the dragon and put the fleshly desires to death.

> Sin was *already* put to death for the believer when he was born again and united to Christ. His sins were nailed to the cross with Christ. But he is *not yet* completely rid of his sin. Christ calls on him to continue to fight the sin that dwells within him every day of his Christian life.

To use an older word, Christ calls on believers to *mortify* the sexual cravings that daily rage within their hearts. When your friend swings that sword at the neck of the dragon, the Spirit is proclaiming, "No! Starve your fleshly desires! Don't give in to this! Kill the evil desires! Give your life to Christ, not to your sexual sin." By God's grace, through Christ's strength, a believer can starve the desires of the flesh and put the beast to death.

How does a believer starve and eventually kill the desires of his flesh? He says no to temptations. He turns his eyes from images of scantily clad or naked women. He distracts himself when he starts thinking about them. He doesn't indulge his lust or fantasies. He gets a software program that helps him to monitor his use of the Internet on his electronic devices. He stops masturbating. He doesn't lie. He hates his sin. He confesses to the Lord. He begs God for mercy. He throws away his rationalizations and self-justifications. He doesn't ignore his guilty pangs and the shame that washes over him. If his conscience sets off an alarm, he pays attention. He chooses obedience. He joins a church and finds rich fellowship. He reminds himself daily of truth. He finds sweet solace in his Savior.

Just looking at this last paragraph may be overwhelming. "That's a lot. How do I keep that all in mind?" Don't be discouraged if this seems too much for you to track. Point to the cross and provide love, support, and solid accountability. God will give you strength to come alongside struggling Christians and help them to do this because the Lord loves them and he wants them to win this battle. If, by the grace of God, they choose faith in Christ and persist in weakening their sin, don't be surprised if the dragon's chokehold loosens over time and no longer rules their lives.

Replace Fleshly Desires with a Greater Affection for Christ

If we stopped right here, the process of changing your friend's desires would be rooted *in her*. But this is a book about God, not your friend. She does need to respond to her difficulties and make a choice. That's her part in the sanctification process. Her most important response is to believe and trust Christ. Deeper change doesn't come from her self-awareness or the steps she takes to put her desires on a diet; rather, the deepest, most sustaining transformation comes when she abides in Christ and is united to him. "Whoever abides in me and I in him, he it is that bears much fruit, for apart from me you can do nothing" (John 15:5). *Abiding* means being spiritually united to Christ—he loves your friend, and she trusts in, hopes in, and loves Christ in return. She lives with her life oriented around Jesus.

Christ came to earth and loved us by giving up his life. He took the initiative in our relationship. We love him because he first loved

168

us (see 1 John 4:19). As we persist in that love and continue to abide in him, our good desires and affections for Christ grow.

Much has been made of Thomas Chalmers's sermon "The Expulsive Power of a New Affection." The basic idea is that, when a believer's adoration of Christ consumes his life, as he hides in Christ and lets Christ become the ruling desire on the throne of his heart, his lesser affections are expelled. Hence, Christ-oriented desires have an expulsive force. They are, in fact, the most powerful desires in the entire universe.

Here's what Chalmers has to say:

> Seldom do any of our habits or flaws disappear by a process of extinction or by the force of mental determination. But what cannot be normally destroyed may be dispossessed; the only way to dispossess the heart of an old affection is by the expulsive power of a new one. . . . The heart's desire for one particular object may be conquered, but its desire to have some object of absolute love is unconquerable. It is only when admitted into the number of God's children through faith in Jesus Christ that the spirit of adoption is poured out on us; it is then and only then, that the heart, brought under the mastery of one great predominant affection, is delivered from the tyranny of all its former desires, and the only way that deliverance is possible.[4]

Thus, the believer's repentance and mortification of sin (and lustful desires) are driven by his greater affection and adoration for Christ. They are powered by his faith and his abiding in Christ.[5]

Revive Good and Healthy Sexual Desires

If a believer's disordered desires for porn have been starved, and eventually killed, and a love for Christ has returned and expelled his disordered desires, the only thing left to do is to revive his good and healthy sexual desires. This is possible through his union with Christ.

George came to me (Deepak) for help. When we started, the problem was that George had lost his awe of Christ long ago. His gospel affection sat in the distance in his rearview mirror. I had the privilege of watching George's life transform as he joined our church community, committed to spiritual disciplines, built solid friendships, and started to open up to me and others about the internal workings of his heart and desires.

What changed? Christ rearranged the internal workings of George's heart, his desires, and (eventually) his life, giving him an awe for Christ, love for his Word and his people, affection for eternal things, and faith in the Savior. As George's gospel affections revived and Christ changed his desires, George nobly fought his sin and starved out his carnal desires, and the war in his heart slowly moved in a more holy and healthy direction. Holy desires for his Savior led him to holy living that was filled with obedience, faithfulness, love, trust, and hope.

Humanly speaking, we must train former porn strugglers to recognize and appreciate what God values. As disciplers, we distinguish between the bad and the good, and we hold out what is truly good and godly. At first, George said, "I can't tell what's truly beautiful." His struggle with pornography had distorted his perspective on sex. Because he had confused healthy sexual desire for his pornified desires, he couldn't tell what was good. So we used the objective standard of God's Word to guide our conversations. Not only did Scripture tell us what are bad desires, but it also laid out good and healthy sexual desires.

What then happened? What was revived in George was a recognition of what is good, right, true, and beautiful. (We explore this more in chapter 21.) George's dehumanizing view of women was killed off, and he began to appreciate Christian sisters for their godly value rather than pornifying and objectifying them. Alongside his pure and healthy perspective on women in our church sprang up a healthy desire for a wife and for sexual intimacy with her. He began to desire a godly, self-sacrificial wife who was also sexually attractive.

Let God train your friend's desires. Help your friend to value what God values. Spiritual disciplines of reading the Word and praying, sitting under weekly preaching, engaging in conversations and life-on-life discipling with mature Christians, participating in the Lord's Supper—all these, plus many more—serve as a fertile training ground in which your friend's heart can be shaped and pointed in a heavenward, Christ-honoring direction. They help him to adopt healthy desires for marriage and sexual intimacy and to take ownership of them.

Reflect: What does the person you're helping want? What does he desire? Are his desires healthy or confused? Can you help him to see the disordered and ruling desires in his life?

Act: Talk with your friend about his inordinate and ruling desires. See if you can help him to grow in his awareness of bad desires and encourage him to repent of those things. Whenever possible, point to the cross and pray for a revival of his affections for Christ. Fan the smoldering embers of his healthy and godly desires.

17

RECOVERING AFTER A FALL

How could I help Tom? . . . What was going on in the days or hours
before he stumbled? What about how he (mis)handled the days and
weeks after a fall? Why did his whole approach to life seem like so
much complicated machinery for managing moral failure?
—*David Powlison,* Making All Things New

For the righteous falls seven times and rises again,
but the wicked stumble in times of calamity.
—*Proverbs 24:16*

Trey feels the pull again. He opens his laptop, tempted to go for it
one more time. "What the heck," he thinks. He has already messed
up once; he may as well go all-out and look at more. He spends
twenty minutes watching porn videos, then shuts the laptop with
a mixture of disgust, self-hatred, and sadness. "I just can't keep
doing this. How could I have done this again?" He is confused and
discouraged. "Why did I keep looking at porn and masturbating?
Why can't I control it?" The pleasure and payoff feel so good in the
moment, but every single time he gives in to temptation, he feels
regret and shame over returning to this filth.

Overwhelmed with shame, Trey resolves to cover up his tracks.
He clears his cache, scrubbing his browsing history, as is his normal
practice. As he goes through his ritual, a nagging feeling deep inside
tells him that he shouldn't keep doing this. A myriad of questions
and thoughts swirl through his mind:

How long will I struggle with this?

Why can't I get over it?

Is looking at porn really worth it?

What's wrong with a little porn here and there? It's not hurting anyone.

Maybe I'm not really a believer, and that's why I can't fight this sin.

If people knew I was involved in this, they would be so disgusted with me.

Will I ever get over this?

Can I change?

What if God doesn't forgive me this time around?

What if I have viewed too much pornography?

After Trey messes up, he is tempted to wallow in shame and self-condemnation, confess to a friend, and white-knuckle his way through the next few days. But is that the best way out of his problems? Solomon writes, "He who trusts in himself is a fool, but one who walks in wisdom will be safe" (Prov. 28:26 BSB). Wisdom is grounded in fearing the Lord (see Prov. 1:1–4) and living according to God's Word. Does Trey know what is wise?

Trey represents scores of young men and women we have met and counseled through the years. Although much of our advice in this book is preventative, we also need to figure out what to do after a mess-up. After all, it is more than likely to happen. Do you and your friend have a plan? What do you do after your friend falls . . . yet again?

The heart of what we're recommending in this chapter is not a haphazard, guilt-inducing approach to the aftermath of a fall but a redemptive, God-honoring four-part plan.

ADDRESS (MOMENTARY) ATHEISM

All sin essentially grows out of our functional unbelief in God— in who he is and what he has done for us. In the moment of temptation, the struggler knocks the Lord from the throne of her life and sets up a god of her own choice: pleasure, relief, happiness, comfort, security. What can be done to address her momentary atheism?

Run to Christ

A struggler's first move after falling into sin should be to run to Christ. *Faith* is the word written across the starting line.

This may seem counterintuitive to the struggler, since God is perhaps the last person she wants to turn to, but therein lies the problem. Think of the Prodigal Son in Luke 15. Verse 17 tells us that "when [the son] came to himself" (or, the NIV says, "when he came to *his senses*")—that is, when he woke up to the painful reality of his pitiful plight—he realized that the best thing he could do was return to his father and confess his sin.

What does Jesus then tell us? When the son was a long way off, the father saw him and, filled with compassion, ran to him. The father ran to the son. Just pause and think about that for a second— Jewish fathers who are wearing long robes and have been shamed by their sons do *not* run to them. Not unless they are merciful and rejoicing over the return of their long-lost wayward sons. The son goes back to the father, and the father runs to the son. If you run back to God, he will come to you (see James 4:8).

God stands ready to hear your struggling friend's confession and listen to it. He's waiting for her to return. Consider Isaiah's words as he calls Israel to repentance:

> Behold, the Lord's hand is not shortened, that it cannot save,
>   or his ear dull, that it cannot hear;
> but your iniquities have made a separation
>   between you and your God,
> and your sins have hidden his face from you
>   so that he does not hear. (Isa. 59:1–2)

As a discipler, address the separation that sin creates between the struggler and God. God stands ready to hear and save if a sinner confesses her sin, repents of it, and trusts God. Plead with your friend to return to God as her refuge, rock, and fortress (see Ps. 46:1; 62:8). There is an ironclad promise from God that when she confesses, he is "faithful and just to forgive" her sins and "to cleanse [her] from all unrighteousness" (1 John 1:9).

Remember God's Character

Right after a fall, a struggling believer may doubt God and wonder if she can really change her situation. She may think things like "I can't change" or "I won't change." Under the surface of these thoughts are unbelief and doubts about God's character: "This is such a mess, and I'm so far gone that God can't clean it up." Your friend thinks her life is beyond God's power to change her.

What is God like to this porn struggler? Is he a mean tyrant, a chastiser? Is the Lord a distant, removed, uncaring God? Does your friend think, "God has forgotten about me"? Or maybe your friend thinks God is good and loving but neither of those attributes apply specifically to his own life. "I know God is good, but he's not good *to me.*"

Another way to address unbelief is to remind a believer of the nature of the God she is sinning against. Unbelief leads her to think wrongly about God, so she needs help to think rightly. In the aftermath of a fall, your friend needs to grab hold of three important facets of God's character in order to reorient herself to the Lord: he is holy, loving, and forgiving. Help your friend to remember that

- *God is holy* (see 1 Peter 1:16). The Hebrew word *holy* means "set apart" or "separate." When we say God is holy, we're saying he is set apart from sin. He's not tainted by it like we are. He's perfect in all his character because sin doesn't affect or change him. Just as God is holy, so also struggling believers are called to lives of purity and holiness (see 1 Peter 1:16). There is no middle ground. A believer should be marked by a growth in godliness. We are to look more and more like our Savior as we walk in the power of the Holy Spirit (see Gal. 5:16).
- *God is loving* (see Lam. 3:31–33). God's love means that he "eternally gives of himself to others."[1] Fundamental to Christianity is a self-sacrificial other-centeredness. Christ gave up his life for us, which is the ultimate testament of one person's love for another. For the guilty and ashamed, to know that they are loved gives hope where there is often none.

176

- *God is forgiving* (see Ps. 32:1–2). Like a compassionate father (see Luke 15), the Lord shows forgiving grace. He is eager and waits for his children. His mercies are new every day. The Lord desires that we come to him in humility and repentance. He casts our sins into the depths of the sea.

As you disciple your friend, it is important that you hold out all three of these characteristics of God. Take out holiness, and you get a God who is kind and sentimental but not concerned about how your friend lives his life. Take out loving or forgiving, and God is austere and demanding without understanding—your friend will be overwhelmed with guilt and shame and will never feel like he can be restored.

ADDRESS ACCESSIBILITY

Your attempts to prevent or slow down your friend's access to pornography—like using a software monitoring program, closing off the app store, and carefully monitoring whatever browser he uses—create a wall. If your friend has fallen, that means there is a crack in the wall—an access point that needs to be closed. If you (or your friend) ignore the crack, later, in a weak moment, your friend will access pornography again. Have no doubt about it, he'll fall again. We can almost guarantee it.

So when your friend falls, you should immediately think, "We need to close that crack." Reevaluate your struggling friend's access to pornography. Check what he's doing with *all* his electronic devices. Don't make any assumptions that he's okay in this area. He probably needs your help.

Pinpoint the Troublesome Open Access Point

Ask your friend questions to figure out where the problem is. Remember that the access points we deal with are *external*—we shut down access to the Internet on a phone, computer, or tablet so that strugglers can no longer view images or videos.

- Where were you when you viewed the pornography? What were you doing? What happened right beforehand?
- What steps were taken previously to remove your access and to construct boundaries to prevent you from viewing pornography?
- Tell me about all your access points to pornography. Did you leave any open access points on your phone, laptop, or device? If you did, why did you do that? Were you planning to sin?
- Do you have access to a phone, laptop, or device that you have not told me about? Have you been hiding it?
- How are you going to cut off access? What active steps do you need to take to close off any cracks in your boundary wall?

Remember that some of the problems we encounter are *internal*, not external. We can also ask questions geared around the heart, getting at the struggler's thoughts and feelings.

- What were you wrestling with in your heart—fear, anger, disappointment, grief, stress, or something else?
- What were you thinking before, during, and after?
- Did your efforts to get around your accountability measures involve deception? Did you lie to me or anyone else?
- How did you feel right after the fall? How do you feel now?

Why are we asking not only about the circumstances and context of the sinful behavior but also about the war in the struggler's heart? Because we know that ultimately the struggler's war to stop porn addiction is fought in his heart, in the context of a loving community, as he keeps his eyes set on Christ. It is not won through a simple change in circumstances or behavior.

Close the Access Point

Once you've asked your friend enough questions to understand his access point to pornography, challenge him to make changes. He'll need to turn over unfiltered devices or make adjustments to devices that he's holding on to. Your goal is to close the cracks in the leaking wall. If Colin has a phone on which he accessed porn last night, we would help him to make adjustments to his phone—to set up restrictions, remove unmonitored web browsers and apps with embedded browsers, and shut down the application store. Getting Colin to close the cracks in the boundary wall gets us out ahead of any other possible incidents.

As a discipler, don't ignore these practical steps. Taking time to show the struggler how to shut down access is a *big* help. Often I (Deepak) will say, "Let's set up everything right now." I'll either take time right then to make all the adjustments to the struggler's phone with him there, or I'll ask him to make the adjustments within twenty-four hours and to notify me that he's done all that we've agreed.

Follow Up

If you don't make changes to a struggler's firewall right away, then you are left to follow up with her. A common mistake disciplers make is to pinpoint an open access point, figure out how to close it, and even ask the struggler to commit to doing so—but not to check later on to see whether she has or not. A sinner has too many incentives to not make changes. Mark down the action items that emerge from your conversation, give the believer enough time to make changes, and follow up to see if she has acted on your counsel.

What if you check in and your friend hasn't made any changes? Then have a conversation that moves beyond circumstances or behavior and digs into his heart motives. For example, laziness, shame, or fear may be stopping him from taking action.

Clinton and I (Jonathan) worked through his porn struggle, and he readily agreed that he should put a software monitoring program on his work computer. But when I checked a week later, I found out he hadn't done it. I probed a little. It turned out that he needed to get permission to load the software onto his work computer, and the IT person was a woman. Clinton was too embarrassed to talk with her about his porn problem. I challenged Clinton to face his fear for the sake of his holiness, and he did.

179

ADDRESS ANONYMITY

Anonymity is a state of being unknown to other people. The guilt and shame of an addiction drive strugglers into anonymity—into being unknown by others and hidden from them. To recover, therefore, the struggler must become known.

Anonymity fosters an isolated lifestyle, and isolation is dangerous. That's why anonymity is such a big problem. Be aware of how pornography struggles can pull a believer away from the very things she needs: (1) God himself and (2) God's wisdom that is made available through God's people. How do you, as a discipler, know this is happening? By being engaged with her life, having honest conversations, and asking thoughtful questions.

The delusion of sin is for a struggler to think, like Adam and Eve, that she can hide from God. In her guilt and shame, she runs away from the Lord. Yet that's foolish: God sees and knows all (see Rom. 2:16). Nothing is hidden from his eyes. Your struggling friend is never left on her own. God is right there with her. She can't isolate herself from God, and it's foolish of her to even consider it.

The basic movement of faith is for a believer to leave the darkness and move toward the light. To borrow a phrase from Edward Welch, the struggling believer must *go public*.[2] She needs to honestly bring her life out into the light. Those who follow Christ should never be unknown or isolated from fellow believers in their own local church.

What would it take for your friend to go public? Doing so means more than just quickly confessing sin. Our goal is to get a believer to move away from anonymity and put her entire life under the loving authority of more mature believers.

Consider a few guidelines to help a believer to move out of isolation and into loving community:

- Encourage the struggler to move toward a trustworthy, loving, maturing Christian. Even better, she should find a few. Who does your friend know in her church? What names come to mind?

- Encourage your friend to be the one to reach out and initiate conversations with you or another discipler. She shouldn't make her disciplers hunt her down. That shows she is not adequately motivated to deal with the problem.
- Help her to speak honestly and forthrightly. She shouldn't use vague language, like "I kinda messed up." Instead, she should be straightforward, blunt, and specific: "I was tempted by unexpected Internet access and fell into pornography again."
- Encourage her to tell others in her life what steps she has taken to address her relationship with God and her open access to pornography.
- Ask her how you can pray for her and then pray for her right there if possible.

A church in which the community of believers learns to be honest about sin, humble about input and correction, and eager to engage with wise disciplers becomes a beacon of light to the world (see Eph. 3:10).

Christ died to save us from our selfish desires (see 2 Cor. 5:14) and to bring us into the family of God (see Rom. 8:14–17; Gal. 4:6–7). For those who have faith, anonymity and isolation are no longer an option.

ADDRESS APPETITE

Once you have addressed the struggler's temporary atheism, access points to pornography, and anonymity, go back and reexamine what he wanted when he fell. What motivated him to move toward pornography? What desires were behind this incident?

First, look at *inordinate* desires—desires that are out of proportion with what is good. On his thirtieth birthday, Morgan despaired over the fact that he was still single and slipped into a pity party. For a few hours on a Saturday afternoon, his sense of being alone in the world, his disappointment in God for not giving him a spouse, and his despair over possibly never getting married loomed so large that he started to scheme about how to satisfy himself. His pity party, despair, and disappointment took his healthy desire to be married and grew it to idolatrous proportions. What quickly emerged was a disordered and disproportionate desire.

Second, look at *ruling* desires. A sense of entitlement led Morgan to begin to demand something for his misery. With time, his demands turned into an outright disregard for God. "God doesn't care anymore, so I'm going to do something about this." His demand and his disregard for God contributed to his desire's becoming a ruling desire. He looked at pornography and masturbated soon afterward.

Morgan was humble about his problem, and he sought out help from a few men in his church. As Morgan's fight against pornography became better, his appetite for porn shrank and he experienced more periods of purity. But when fear, anger, despair, and disappointment crept in at certain moments, his appetite grew again and created the perfect incentive for him to fall back into sin.

Armed with knowledge about these desires and specific questions to ask the struggler about them, you will be able to get at these appetites. Consider the following points:

- *People overrun by carnal desires tend to lie.* What lies and rationalizations have been rolling around in the struggler's mind and heart?

- *People overrun by desires live for the moment.* What consequences, future plans, or perspectives does the believer need to be reminded of?

- *Not everyone is self-aware enough to know what desires are motivating him.* Ask the struggler and dig around in his heart to see what you can discover. (Chapters 6 and 16 give guidance on how to do this.)

- *Disproportionately large desires need to be pared down and starved until they return to their proper weight and importance.* What changes does the struggler need to make, what thoughts does he need to own, and what perspectives does he need to readjust to make his inordinate desires more ordinate?

- *It is not enough for the struggler to simply say no to the fleshly desires.* We must equip and exhort those we are caring for to cultivate an appetite for Christ and holiness! What affections and cravings for Christ does the struggling Christian need to cultivate and prioritize so that he buys less into what the world is saying? What practical implications does that have for his life? How can you encourage him to train his values to line up with God's values?

Too often, conversations about pornography are more *prohibitive* than *invitational.* Christ *invites* and beckons struggling believers to lose themselves in him. To follow him with their whole hearts. To glorify him with their bodies. To experience his love and mercy.

HOPE AFTER A FALL

Keep these things in mind the next time your friend comes to you after a fall. No plan is ever foolproof, but as you give attention to these four *As* (momentary atheism, access, anonymity, and appetite), you increase the likelihood that the struggling believer will be better equipped to face the next round of temptation. He doesn't have to give up hope that his addiction will ever change. With Christ, and your help, real change is possible.

Reflect: Think about the last time you met with your friend after a fall. What did you do? Which one of these four *As* did you leave out? How can you adjust your approach the next time your friend comes to you?

Act: The next time your friend comes to you after a fall, pray through these four *As* together. Then talk through each of the *As* one by one.

18

UNDERSTANDING GUILT AND SHAME

There is nothing more effective *than guilt to get people to obey God's standards, and nothing less* efficacious *in sanctifying them to God.*
—*Bryan Chapell,* Holiness by Grace

No condemnation now hangs over the head of those who are "in" Jesus Christ. For the new spiritual principle of life "in" Christ lifts me out of the old vicious circle of sin and death.
—*Romans 8:1,* J. B. Phillips New Testament

Lucas slumps into the overstuffed chair in the corner of your office for his 10:00 a.m. appointment. He looks a bit disheveled, and he fails to make eye contact when you go to greet him. He stares at the floor.

After opening in prayer, you inquire, "Well, how are things going?"

"I messed up again and looked at pornography," Lucas mumbles. "I don't know why. I almost didn't come in today because I was so embarrassed to see you after all you've tried to do to help me."

If you've been helping a struggler for more than a few weeks, you've probably had a conversation just like this. The unevenness of sanctification—some good days followed by bad falls to temptation; trust in Christ in one moment and despair in the next—is a common mark of those who struggle with addictive behavior. Across the span of their lives, sanctification looks more like a stock market chart than a straight line.

Guilt and shame inevitably complicate a struggler's life. You can't engage an addict without addressing the towers of guilt and shame that are present in almost every conversation, whether acknowledged or not. Guilt and shame are part of the human experience, ever since that fatal day when Adam and Eve were *naked and ashamed,* and nowhere is their presence felt more than in the area of sexual sin. They form formidable barriers to spiritual growth and recovery from a porn addiction, and they must be addressed biblically.

Edward Welch provides the following definitions:

- *Guilt*: Our state of culpability and condemnation before God for our sin. It is the personal conviction of sin for wrong done against God.
- *Shame*: The deep sense that you are unacceptable [to God and others] because of something you did, something done to you, or something associated with you.[1]

To put it another way, guilt plays in the arena of things *you have done* and shame plays in the arena of *who you are.*

Scripture speaks to these two profound human experiences with liberating, heart-soaring, gospel-soaked truth.

A SEXUAL SINNER'S EXPERIENCE OF GUILT

I (Jonathan) have a tendency to drive a bit faster than I should. When I went to college in southern California, I started driving with more frequency and quickly learned that, unless you are driving seventy- or eighty-plus miles an hour, you'll get run off the road. Fast-forward to the slower pace of life in the Midwest. One day I was pulled over by a police officer as I zipped through a school zone. He intoned, "Sir, do you know why I pulled you over?"

Now, in that moment, did I feel shame and embarrassment? Yes, a little bit. As I looked around and watched cars pass me, I slumped lower in my seat, hoping none of my neighbors would see me. However, I more profoundly experienced *guilt.* I knew I had broken a law. There was no excuse. There was no way to get around it. I had been caught, and I was going to be held accountable. (The police officer did not let me off with a warning but instead issued my first speeding ticket!)

So also a porn struggler has a profound sense of guilt right after he's looked at illicit images or videos. As you disciple friends who struggle, you'll hear guilt-ridden language, such as "I shouldn't have done that" or "What I did was wrong." Their experience of guilt can take them down one of two paths.

The Fleshly Path: Guilt Can Lead a Struggler to Self-Loathing and Self-Focus

After a struggler falls, his guilt shifts into full gear, and self-condemnation rages: "You idiot, you fell again." "How could you be a Christian?" He may wallow in self-pity, and his focus narrows to his own doubts, hurts, and momentary despair. "Who cares?" "Why do I keep trying?" What a mess.

The apostle Paul called this "worldly grief" that "produces death" (2 Cor. 7:10). Although the struggler feels bad about what he did, his focus is on himself, not on the fact that he's offended a holy God. Guilt piles on top of guilt when there is no genuine repentance. It creates a pile of self-condemnation larger than the trash heap at the local garbage dump.

The path of worldly grief and sorrow might look like genuine repentance initially, but, as the discipler, you must examine its fruit to discern whether the struggler is experiencing godly or worldly guilt. Just because the struggler has bad feelings or feels guilty about his sin does not mean he has undergone genuine heart change.

Many strugglers are mired in cycles of guilt and condemnation because they believe that their sin is too great to be forgiven by God. In this we see a struggler's functional atheism and the Enemy's insidious deception. Instead of helping him to appreciate the forgiving and merciful nature of God, a struggler's guilt leads him to self-condemning, self-atoning, and self-loathing actions. Even if the struggler confesses, his goal is to alleviate and relieve his experience of guilt rather than to confess his wrongdoing and experience the joy of a restored relationship with God (see Ps. 51:7–12).

As a discipler, you must distinguish between temporary guilt relief and blood-bought guilt removal. Push your friend by asking, "Do you feel bad about what you did, but nothing more? Or do you feel like you've offended a holy God with your sin?"

If your friend hasn't grasped the bigger picture yet, then use these questions to shift his focus off his temporary guilt relief. Help him to understand that his offense is first against God and that what's required of him is genuine repentance. (We saw this in more detail in chapter 9.) If your friend realizes his sin has offended God, he is on a better path.

The Spirit-Driven Path: Guilt Can Lead a Struggler to Acknowledge Sin and Repent

When the Holy Spirit convicts a struggler over the wrong she has done, her Spirit-driven sense of guilt leads her to confession and repentance. "Whoever conceals his transgressions will not prosper, but he who confesses and forsakes them will obtain mercy" (Prov. 28:13). Godly grief over sin leads the struggler to say something. Confession of sin is good for the soul. It acknowledges before God and others that wrong has been done.

But confession is only the first step. Words alone don't work. A porn struggler's grief must become a stepping-stone to genuine repentance. She must turn from empty cisterns of lust, the carnal desires that scream for more, and the selfishness that rules her heart and run to Christ in faith. Moved by the Spirit, the struggler must flee to the Savior because she hopes in his merciful and gracious nature. As she grows in her trust of Christ, she begins to look more like her Savior, who loved and served others and sacrificed and humbled himself to do so.

THE GOSPEL SOLUTION FOR GUILT

One of the most glorious aspects of Christianity is that God offers forgiveness of sin and thus relief for a guilty conscience. With God's forgiveness, our sin is so far removed from us that we are no longer guilty in God's eyes. When we are made righteous before God through Christ, our guilty feelings are taken away in the shadow of the cross. What a glorious thing it is to live with a guilt-free conscience.

I (Deepak) sat with a man yesterday who had fallen again to sexual sin. As I said to him, "On behalf of the Lord, I declare that God has forgiven you through the blood of Christ," tears streamed down his face. His guilt was real and palpable, but the power of the cross is greater than the guilt caused by his reckless sexual sin. Puritan pastor Richard Sibbes wrote, "He is more ready . . . to forgive than you to sin; as there is a continual spring of wickedness in you, so there is a greater spring of mercy in God."[2]

A fleshly reaction to guilt reveals itself in the ongoing selfish and prideful pursuits of a struggler. A Spirit-driven reaction, in stark contrast, is displayed through confession, repentance, and fruits of the Spirit—increasing doses of humility, self-control, love, and even joy.

A SEXUAL SINNER'S EXPERIENCE OF SHAME

Shame is different from guilt. In some ways, it's more pervasive because it touches and affects the very core of who we are—our identity. Shame colors a struggler's past and present and often taints his hopes and dreams for his future. One struggler described his experience of shame as a "cosmic embarrassment before God and others." Welch perceptively notes, "Guilt can be hidden; shame feels like it is always exposed."[3]

Think of some of the ways that shame impacts strugglers:

- A single guy looks at pornography and feels unworthy to pursue a girlfriend until he "gets control of this area of his life."
- A woman masturbates but feels unable to be vulnerable and share her struggle with other women for fear of being judged and gossiped about.
- A married woman has a secret life of pornography, erotic chat rooms, and voyeurism and is afraid and embarrassed to tell her husband.

189

Sexual sinners can experience shame in many different ways. Yet for many strugglers, shame is an amorphous experience. They know they are ashamed, but they don't know how to *biblically* describe their turmoil.

The Bible uses the following concepts to describe the experiences of shame. Believers who commit sexual sin are all too familiar with these four variations of shame.

Shame Concept	Biblical Example	The Struggler's Personal Narrative
Nakedness	Adam and Eve (Gen. 3:7–8)	"I'm vulnerable, exposed, and uncovered."
Rejection or being an outcast	The Samaritan woman (John 4)	"I don't belong. No one wants me here. I'll always be an outsider."
Uncleanliness or contamination	A leper (Mark 1:40–42)	"I'm unworthy and wretched. I'm dirty and worthless."
Failure[4]	Peter (Matt. 26:75)	"I messed up again."

Let's look at these biblical ideas in greater detail. Which one best describes the Christian you are helping?

Naked and Uncovered

The moment Sally appeared, Jack was caught. "I felt embarrassed after Sally walked in. I was looking at naked women on my laptop. She was angry—a white hot, raging, I-could-just-kill-you anger. Her look blazed a hole right through my thick skull. I couldn't make eye contact. I felt naked and exposed. The ugliest parts of me—my carnal lust, my disgust with myself—were right there for her to see."

In the garden of Eden, Adam and Eve partook of the forbidden fruit, and then Moses tells us, "The eyes of both were opened, and they knew that they were naked. And they sewed fig leaves together.

. . . And the man and his wife hid themselves from the presence of the LORD" (Gen. 3:7–8). The first couple covered themselves and hid from God. Why? Because they experienced guilt and shame for their sin. In Genesis 2, there was no sin in the world, so there was no shame. But after sin entered in, shame quickly followed. Adam and Eve's eyes were opened to good and evil, and they personally experienced shame. They knew they were naked, and they felt embarrassed, so they covered themselves.

In the same way, because of his shame, Jack spent months hiding from his wife. It was as if he'd covered himself with fig leaves and hidden behind a bush. In reality, he was hiding not just from her but also from God. When Sally stepped into the room, the fig leaves were ripped off, and Jack's ugliest sins were exposed to her.

Unclean, Contaminated, and Impure

Andrew had a strong sense of being dirty after he acted out. "I looked and felt filthy. The sin that had seemed so attractive and appealing a moment before now left me disgusted and empty. It felt wrong to use the hand that I gratified myself with to shake the hand of a brother or sister at church." As Andrew and other strugglers use words like *filthy*, *dirty*, *empty*, or *disgusting*, they capture their sense of impurity before God and others. Their shame makes them feel horrible about themselves.

In the Old Testament, purification laws kept the unclean from the clean, the impure from the pure.[5] If you touched a carcass (see Num. 5:2), came in contact with a skin disease (see Lev. 13–14), or ate unclean foods (see Lev. 11; Deut. 14), you were unclean. You could not associate with the clean or the pure. An unclean priest approached the sanctuary under threat of divine wrath (see Lev. 15:31; 21:1–24). An unclean layperson couldn't eat the consecrated food (see Lev. 7:20–21) or approach God's tabernacle (see Num. 5:3). The goal of the unclean was to become clean again through purification so they could enter God's holy presence and rejoin Israel's community.

The categories of uncleanliness and impurity show up in the experiences of a porn struggler. As the struggler gets more deeply entrenched in his sexual sin, he has no confidence to approach God, so he comes up with his own self-atonement or purification rites to regain a sense of worthiness or cleanliness. He tries to assuage his sense of shame, which in Andrew's case often came out as self-condemnation. He'd beat up on himself verbally: "I'm an idiot" or "How could I be so stupid as to do it again?"

Outcast

Jacob anguished over his sexual sin: "I feel unworthy of having a godly wife to love. The best I can do is lust after a stranger on my computer screen. Something is wrong with me." Shame made Jacob feel like he didn't deserve marriage. But it also made him feel like he didn't belong at church: "The people at church all look so perfect. No one else struggles like I do." He felt rejected, like an outcast who didn't belong.

Think of the Samaritan woman from John 4. Jews and Samaritans despised one another, so it was shocking that Jesus, a man and a Jew, would talk with her. But why did she come alone to get water in the middle of the day when it was hottest? It seems she avoided other women because of her personal and marital history; the shame of being an outcast was written all over her life.

Failure

Sheila was mad at herself. "I did it again. How can I call myself a Christian and keep doing this?" She felt frustrated that she had given in yet again to her sexual sin. Her sense of failure as a believer was so strong that it made her second-guess her salvation.

As the rooster crowed three times, Peter remembered the words of Jesus: "Before the rooster crows, you will deny me three times" (Matt. 26:75). Peter immediately went out and wept. Just like Sheila, Peter experienced a sense of failure. The gravity of Peter's sin of denying Jesus Christ moved Peter to bitter tears. One can only imagine the sense of failure that accompanied such a denial of the One he professed to love so deeply.

THE GOSPEL SOLUTION FOR SHAME

When helping a shame-filled struggler, we need a message—a gospel message—that is strong enough, rich enough, and deep enough to address the deepest and most cavernous areas of his heart. The paradox of shame is that a struggler gets so distracted by the horizontal (for example, his wife's anger at him for watching pornography) that he loses sight of the greater shame: his sin against a holy God. Yet his deepest shame is his shame before God, not others. He must not be like Adam and Eve, running and hiding from the Lord.

Your friend needs to be confronted with a person who knows her inside and out—every site she has visited, and every person she has lusted after—and who doesn't give up on her. She needs the incarnated Savior, Jesus Christ himself, to reach down into her life and take her shame and guilt upon himself. That's the way Jesus deals with shame. He comes to us, dwells with us, makes his home with us. He shares life with us, and he does not move away from us when things get hard or messy.

Christ covers the naked and exposed. He is the garment that hides their nakedness. God killed an animal to construct coverings for Adam and Eve (see Gen. 3:21). It was his first act of mercy to the first couple. Paired with this is the first gospel promise that the woman's seed would one day crush Satan's head (see Gen. 3:15). This seed is Christ. Jesus would come to earth to cover his people—from the priest with dirty clothes (see Zech. 3:3–5) to the New Testament believers to whom he gave his very righteousness (see 2 Cor. 5:21). Christ would conceal the exposed.

Jesus welcomes the rejected and outcast into God's family and declares that they are the King's children. In John 4, the Samaritan woman's most embarrassing moment must have been when Jesus brought up her sexual history. What an intimate and shameful part of her past! Yet Jesus didn't bring up those details to further shame her. He wanted her to know that men could never ultimately satisfy her. Only Christ could. He welcomed this outcast woman into the loving embrace of his kingdom. Through Christ, the rejected and outcast are justified and adopted into God's family. Those who are lowly are invited into the kingdom of heaven (see Matt. 5:3).

The clean (Jesus) touches the unclean and makes her clean again. Think of the leper in Matthew 8. "If you are willing, make me clean," the leper asked Christ. So often, Jesus spoke and enacted change by the mere power of his words. But slow down the film and notice what happens next. Jesus reaches out and touches the leper. Those around the leper would have said, "What was the use of that? The leper just made Jesus ceremonially unclean." But to think this way is to lose sight of the fact that the One who touched the leper was the Holy One and the Savior of the world. When Jesus touches the unclean, the power in his touch is able to make them clean, holy, and forgiven (see Matt. 8:1–3).[6]

The perfect One gave his righteousness so the person who has failed no longer needs to work out his problem on his own but instead can find rest in the all-sufficient Savior. Can you imagine how Peter felt after he denied Jesus a third time and the rooster crowed? He was loaded down with guilt and shame. And yet Christ's sufficiency in the face of Peter's insufficiency is seen after Jesus's resurrection. In John 21, Jesus asked Peter, "Do you love me more than these?" Then he charged Peter three times to "feed my sheep" (John 21:15–17). The implication is "*If* you love me more than these, *then* feed my sheep." How could that be? How could Christ ask the one who denied him to serve him by taking care of his sheep? Because Christ was righteous and sufficient in a way Peter never could be. If Peter's future ventures depended on himself, then Jesus wouldn't have needed to ask the question. Implied in Jesus's question is a challenge: "You *must* now love me." In light of the suffering Peter would face on Christ's behalf (see John 21:18–19), Peter needed to depend on his Savior to receive all that he needed.

194

The solution for every kind of shame is Christ. David Powlison writes, "[Jesus] enters sympathetically into the totality of human experience. He touches all our sins and all our afflictions. Jesus's mercies make all things new. His grace is a most versatile stain remover. He redeems both the wayward and wounded. . . . He goes to work on us. He works in us for as long as it takes. He does not give up. He will not give up on you."[7] Ask your friend if he trusts in Christ and believes that Christ can take away his shame. Praise the Lord for this amazing grace!

The best place in the world is in God. The sinner must hide in Christ. Christ, "for the joy that was set before him," took on his shame (Heb. 12:2). Glory be to God—he sent a Savior to help the sinner with his shame.

Reflect: What's your experience of guilt and shame? Have you seen the gospel solutions for guilt and shame come to fruition in your own life? The more you personally experience Christ's help for your guilt and shame, the more you can point out this very same hope to others.

Act: Use the biblical categories of shame to examine what variations of shame plague the heart of the struggler you are discipling.

19

UNDERSTANDING AND DISCIPLINING THE BODY

Biblical Christianity may be the most
body-positive religion in the world.
—*Timothy Keller with Kathy Keller,* The Meaning of Marriage

Or do you not know that your body is a temple of the Holy Spirit
within you, whom you have from God? You are not your own, for you
were bought with a price. So glorify God in your body.
—*1 Corinthians 6:19–20*

God made us with *both* bodies and souls. We have an *embodied* existence—physical hearts, blood, spines, neurons, muscles, tissue, organs, skin, bones, and brains. We also have a *spiritual* existence. Your soul is that inner part of you that is eternal and gives you a personal relationship with the Creator whose image you bear.

Your body and soul are seamlessly woven together. In life you can't have one without the other. And to deny either body or soul is to deny reality. You are fearfully and wonderfully made. Much of what we've addressed in this book deals with the soul—with spiritual issues such as faith, repentance, sin, guilt, shame, and hope. But we don't want to make the all-too-common mistake of overly spiritualizing things. We can't ignore the plain fact that we have bodies and those bodies play a role in pornography addictions.

Pornography addictions affect both spirit and body. If we ignore the body, we handicap our ability to help porn strugglers. Over the next few pages, we want to understand how porn affects a struggler's body and how he can discipline and control his body.

THE NEUROCHEMISTRY OF THE BRAIN DURING PORN STRUGGLES

If we put on X-ray glasses and explored what was going on inside a struggling believer, what would we find? Many people have done detailed research on pornography's effect on the body. Some of this research shows why pornography is so potent, and some shows why it is so destructive. What we offer is a brief, lay-friendly guide to a complicated subject.

Our bodies use chemicals, known as *neurotransmitters*, to send messages across the nervous system. They're a bit like Paul Revere riding through town, crying out, "The British are coming!" and our nervous system reacts to their announcement. The neurotransmitter known as dopamine is our bodies' "feel-good" chemical, motivating our pleasure and reward systems. Dopamine kicks in when you drink cold water on a hot day, chomp down on a high-quality steak, or have sex with your spouse. It is essential for sexual arousal and sexual drive because it's what gets a person excited and what helps him to enjoy pleasure. Although dopamine can serve a good purpose, unfortunately it is also activated in the brain by the sight of pornography.[1]

When pornography is repeatedly used, it changes the viewer's brain. In his book *Wired for Intimacy*, William Struthers describes continual porn consumption as affecting neural pathways, much like when hundreds of people walk the exact same grass pathway. Under the stress of all those stomping feet, a dirt road is formed. So also the continual firing and overuse of dopamine changes certain neural pathways to become automatic if given enough time. "They become the automatic pathway[s] through which interactions with women are routed. . . . All women become potential porn stars" for men who view porn regularly.[2]

When a person repeatedly consumes pornography, there is a decrease of dopamine available in the brain, and the dopamine cells start to shrink. That creates a state of craving: the struggler wants more in order to boost his dopamine levels—just to feel normal.[3] Herein lies the addictive quality of this problem—the believer's body is screaming for more pleasure, so it demands more pornography.

Pornography use changes the brain in other ways. Drug addiction and other addictions (such as to food and pornography) are shown to cause atrophy, or shrinking, of the brain's frontal lobes. These frontal lobes "are important in judgment. . . . If the brain were a car, the frontal lobes would be the brakes. These lobes have important connections to the pleasure pathways, so pleasure can be controlled."[4] When pornography is repeatedly consumed, the "brake pads" of the brain wear out, and "the person [becomes] impaired in his ability to process the consequences of acting out in addiction."[5] This is the neurochemical basis for the problem we discussed in chapter 12—the inability of the struggling believer, when he acts out with pornography, to see beyond the moment and to comprehend the consequences for his future.[6]

Pornography use can cause significant changes and damage to the brain, but mirror neurons show why pornography is so powerful in the first place. The brain cells known as *mirror neurons* are called "monkey see, monkey do" neurons. If you watch a person throw a baseball, eat an apple, or chop wood, these neurons activate in your brain. You use them to adopt the other person's point of view and prove that you are capable of doing the same activity.[7] Scientists say these neurons are key for human imitation, allowing us to mirror the actions of others.[8]

Keeping in mind what mirror neurons do, you can imagine what happens when pornography is consumed. As a man watches a pornographic video, his brain "reacts [as though he] were the person engaged in the sexual act. Viewing a pornographic movie creates a neurological experience whereby a person vicariously participates in what he is watching. . . . He can neurologically identify with the performers in the video. . . . To deal with the arousal it creates, the brain mirrors and heightens the arousal, causing even more sexual tension. The sexual drive is fueled even further and screams for an outlet."[9] It's no surprise then that masturbation typically follows pornography use. The viewer relieves the sexual tension by facilitating a release of the pent-up arousal.

What we've described are just a few component parts of what happens inside the brain of a person who is consuming pornography. What we see is that pornography use has a discernable and damaging effect on the body. This shows what we're up against as we help believers to fight porn addictions. There is much more that could be said, but our goal has been to give a mere sampling of the inner workings of the brain and of neurons.

AROUSAL, DISCIPLINING THE BODY, AND SELF-CONTROL

All porn strugglers battle with self-control and bodily urges. Idolatrous heart cravings hook physical bodies. When strugglers are enslaved to pornography, the idolatrous cravings of their hearts and the physical desires of their bodies feed off one another in an endless cycle, constantly demanding more.[10] The body is stirred awake as the eyes take in illicit images or the mind recalls explicit videos. Mirror neurons fire; dopamine runs across synapses, transmitting messages ("There's an opportunity for pleasure!"); heart rate increases; palms become sweaty or cold; eyes dilate; the groin tingles; and muscles tense.[11] The addict descends into a pit of indulging his desires.

"Satan enters this drama because he has a special interest in exploiting the body's natural needs and desires. If something feels physically good, you can bet he will try to take advantage of it." —Edward T. Welch[12]

Satan is especially good at appropriating our God-given physical pleasures and convincing us to use them for selfish ends. At the same time as the body is aroused, the internal heart war is raging. The struggler wavers as she is tempted to indulge her cravings; she experiences shame and guilt, lies and rationalizations, and self-condemnation. Sadly, her bodily arousal and stirred heart can end in her willful choice to act out in sexual sin—intimacy, intercourse, or masturbation.

Is the war with the body a lost cause? Not at all. We've criticized a white-knuckling approach—a struggler's attempt to control and overcome powerful desires by relying on his own sheer willpower and strength. But though we disapprove of this approach, that doesn't mean the Bible is silent about self-control. For example, the apostle Paul writes,

> *Every athlete exercises self-control in all things.* They do it to receive a perishable wreath, but we an imperishable. So I do not run aimlessly; I do not box as one beating the air. But *I discipline my body* and *keep it under control.* (1 Cor. 9:25–27)

Although Paul commends athletic self-control and discipline of the body, when he talks about saying no to ungodliness and worldly passions and living a self-controlled life, he roots his discussion not in our moral self-reformation but in God's grace to us through Jesus Christ. Jesus "redeem[ed] us from all wickedness . . . to purify for himself a people that are his very own" (Titus 2:14 NIV). A believer's ability to hold off bodily demands and heart cravings is rooted not in himself but in what Christ has done for him.

Faith in Christ is the gasoline that powers the engine of self-control. If we trust in him, we grow to be more like him, and greater self-control is both a gift of the Father (see 2 Tim. 1:7) and a fruit of the Holy Spirit (see Gal. 5:23).[13] Through a believer's faith, the same power that raised Christ from the dead works to help the believer to restrain his body, discipline his cravings, and obediently pursue a pure life (see Eph. 1:19–20). As described in the Pastoral Epistles, mature leaders model this kind of self-control of the body, cravings, and anything else that attempts to take over and wreak havoc (see Titus 1:8–9).

How can a person discipline her body? While there are a variety of practical ways to do this, consider one example—verbalizing a struggle. Rather than being a passive victim who is overrun by her carnal desires for pornography, anyone can reactivate her frontal cortex by verbalizing the dynamics of her struggle. Picture a believer who starts thinking about looking at pornography ("I deserve some pleasure after a hard day"). Her body starts getting aroused, and she starts getting emotionally charged up. She says to herself out loud, "I know that's a trigger, and I'm not going to engage it." "I feel my body ramping up, and I need to call a friend for help." "I'm going to ask God right now to slow this down." A few words alone won't defeat the problem, but this is a microstep in heading off a potential problem.[14] Often a person is passive because they are overwhelmed by the cravings and don't know how to respond. Verbalizing the struggle helps this person to consciously acknowledge the problem ("I know that's a trigger") and also what can be done about it ("I'm not going to engage it" or "I need to call a friend").

HOW DOES THIS CHANGE WHAT YOU DO?

The question is, What difference does this make for you? How does this knowledge of the body help us in our discipling of believers who struggle with pornography and masturbation? Consider two important facts.

God Can Change Anyone and Anything

In sanctification, God works by creating alternate neurological pathways. Abstinence—also known as "making no provision for the flesh" (Rom. 13:14)—can make a difference.[15] Matt Fradd affirms this: "Porn can and does hijack the neurocircuits of the brain, but with time and effort, the brain can be given space to heal itself."[16] No part of the human brain is beyond Christ's lordship. He's King over every neurotransmitter and neuron. No addictive behavior—absolutely none—is beyond God's grace to redeem, no matter how bad it is or how long it has occurred. The supernatural work of God transforms the metaphysical world because God runs it all. It bows to his every command. Nothing is out of reach of the throne room of heaven.

As disciplers, we can't operate as if the body—or Satan's taking advantage of bodily cravings for dopamine—will set the pace for the person's recovery. If we believe as disciplers that Christ is the Lord of our bodies, we let our beliefs set the agenda for our discipling. Your hope that Christ can change anything should spill over into your discipling conversations.

The Changes May Take Time

That said, long-term sinful patterns foster more deeply ingrained habits. Long-term sin rewires our neurochemistry. A believer's sexual history reveals how much sexual sin has rewritten his brain's neural pathways. If your friend tells you he's struggled since he was a teenager (or even younger), a lot of internal change will have accompanied his sin. His habits are more ingrained and his dopamine craving more intense because of the internal rewiring. The longer and more frequent his battle with porn, the harder it will be for him to reverse the patterns. (Note we said "harder"—not "impossible.") The more years a person has made provision for his flesh, the more difficult the fight will be (see Rom. 13:14).

As a discipler, you'll need to take a long-term perspective on fighting this sexual sin. Complete freedom from pornography won't come in a few days or weeks but will take much longer. You must proactively reset the expectations of the struggler by articulating a long-term perspective: "Since you struggled with porn from an early age, your habits are more ingrained. Change won't happen overnight. It's going to take a while to find freedom from this sin, so you'll need to be patient as we fight this together." (We'll think much more about adopting a big-picture and long-term view in chapter 20.) Therapists Wendy Maltz and Larry Maltz write,

> Porn's power to produce experiences of excitement, relaxation, and escape from pain make it highly addictive. Over time you can come to depend on it to feel good and require it so you don't feel bad. Cravings, preoccupations, and out-of-control behavior with using it can become commonplace. Porn sex can become your greatest need. If you have been using porn regularly to "get high," withdrawal from porn can be as filled with agitation, depression, and sleeplessness

as detoxing from alcohol, cocaine, and other hard drugs. In fact, people in porn recovery take an average of eighteen months to heal from the damage to their dopamine receptors alone.[17]

Picture a huge cruise liner and a little tugboat. If they have to make a 180 degree turn in the water, which one turns around faster? The tugboat. The cruise ship is much bigger and has much more momentum built up in one direction. It must take a wider turn to reverse direction. So also for the person whose struggle has been long-term. The habits are more ingrained, so he or she will need to take a long-term view of the fight against sin.

WITH GOD NOTHING IS IMPOSSIBLE

It would be incorrect to reduce us to a bunch of neurons. We're more than a conglomeration of neurons with brains. We're living, breathing image bearers of God the Almighty. We're made to be like God and imitate him (see Eph. 5:1)—to love, create, exercise justice, show mercy, and so on. If we are anything less than God's image bearers, we're nothing more than mere animals without souls. If you believe that, you've bought into a lie.

The neurochemistry behind a porn addiction can never be used as an excuse to indulge in sin. Let's say someone tells you, "I can't help it. This is how I'm wired." You should respond, "It may be true that you're wired this way, but that doesn't provide an excuse. And even better, God can work in you to defeat this sin and rewire your brain!"

Reflect: Do you have a balanced view of how bodily urges, human willpower, and God's help fit together? Or have you (in the past) ignored the impact of the body on porn struggles?

Act: If you've never done so, ask about your friend's sexual history. Patiently listen and ask questions along the way, but be careful not to shame or scrutinize your friend. Your goal is to learn how long and in-depth the fight against sexual sin has been, so you can understand how much internal change has occurred in your friend's body.

20

GETTING A GLIMPSE OF THE BIG PICTURE

My barn having burned down, I can now see the moon.
—*Mizuta Masahide, untitled poem*

*And we know that for those who love God all things work together
for good, for those who are called according to his purpose.*
—*Romans 8:28*

In times of trouble and suffering, strugglers often lose perspective. They easily get overwhelmed in their spiritual journey. They ask questions like "Is this really worth it?" or "When am I ever going to be done with sexual temptation?" or "Will this ever get better?" David Powlison writes, "In *principle*, the idea of sexual renewal [is] very simple. Here's darkness, here's light. Here's bad, here's good. Here's being dirty, here's being clean. But in *process*, it's a lifetime."[1] Because this process lasts a lifetime, strugglers can become overwhelmed as they lose sight of who God is and how he is acting in their lives.

The goal of this chapter is to talk about the bigger picture of a struggler's life. Far too often, a struggler and discipler can be short-sighted. Because of his sin, a struggler loses perspective about what God is doing. Because a discipler can get discouraged by the lack of progress in his friend's life, he also loses perspective.

We want to help you to grab hold of three bigger-picture perspectives that will lend strength to the struggler as she seeks to persevere in this fight. Our aim is to help you to grasp these perspectives so that you can pass them on.

GOD USES EVENTS IN A STRUGGLER'S LIFE
TO MAKE HIM MORE LIKE CHRIST

David Powlison talks about sinning as *self-inflicted suffering*.[2] To use the apostle James's language, porn struggles are "trials of various kinds" (James 1:2). A struggler's foolish choice results in difficult consequences for his life. Tim looks at porn; his wife catches him. She's disappointed and angry for the next week. Tim's foolishness brought about his suffering.

Now pull the lens back and get a wider glimpse of Tim's life. We know that God uses all things—even our sinful choices—for the good of those who love him (see Rom. 8:28). Think in terms of Joseph and his brothers. Though Joseph's brothers sinned by selling him into slavery, God used their foolishness for his glory and their greater good. "[They] meant evil against me, but God meant it for good" (Gen. 50:20). The Lord doesn't tempt us (see James 1:13), and he is not to blame for Tim's foolish choice to look at pornography. Yet Romans 8:28 and Genesis 50:20 show us that a struggler's foolishness is not beyond God's control of the universe.

In the book of James, the Lord gives us a glimpse into what he is doing in and through our trials and situations:

> Count it all joy, my brothers and sisters, when you meet trials of various kinds, for you know that the testing of your faith produces steadfastness. And let steadfastness have its full effect, that you may be perfect and complete, lacking in nothing. (James 1:2–4)

Here the apostle James gives us striking clarity as to why we go through what we go through: *the testing of your faith produces steadfastness . . . that you may be perfect and complete!* In other words, even a struggler's foolish choices are used by God *so that* he might become spiritually mature in Christ. The trials we endure are not haphazard; they are not random tests by a disconnected deity. Our trials are meant to form us into the image of Christ.

Does the person you are helping understand this? Has he lost sight of the big picture? Or does he see the bigger picture of who God is and what he is doing in his life?

Here's the first bigger-picture perspective we offer you: God is overseeing the events of a struggler's life so that he will become increasingly mature. The Lord uses the process of sanctification, over the long-term, to make this struggler more like Christ.

OUR FINAL REDEMPTION IS COMING

I (Deepak) had a friend who would go to a local bookstore and read the first and last chapter of a book before he committed himself to reading the entire book. He wanted to know the end of the story before he read the whole book.

In the same way, we as disciplers need to help our friends to keep their eyes set on the final redemption. Why? Because if a struggler knows the end of the story, that will help him *right now* to persevere through his trials. His more immediate trials don't define him. Rather, he'll be like Christ when Jesus returns.

The apostle John describes this need for perspective:

Beloved, we are God's children now, and what we will be has not yet appeared; but we know that when he appears we shall be like him, because we shall see him as he is. And everyone who thus hopes in him purifies himself as he is pure. (1 John 3:2–3)

Here is the vantage point John offers us: hoping in our final redemption has a sanctifying or purifying effect on our souls (see also 1 Peter 1:13). John says, "Listen, we don't know exactly how things are going to turn out for us, but we do know that when Jesus comes back, we will be like him when we see him! And if you have this hope, it can sanctify your soul."

Writing those words brings tears to our eyes. Oh, the hope we have in Christ even in the midst of all our brokenness and sin. We are God's beloved children, and he has purposed before the beginning of time to complete this work of redemption in our lives and in the lives of the people we are helping. This is a promise that you, the discipler, should grab hold of and be ready to pass on to your friend.

GOD-GIVEN PROGRESS HAS BEEN MADE

Sin—especially sexual sin—blinds a sinner. If you drive down a California highway, you'll see mountains spread across the landscape in the distance. Imagine you are standing at the base of a mountain, with your face only inches away from the rock and weeds up to your knees. All you can see is what is in front of you—the plain rock of this one mountain. That's what sexual sin does—it makes you lose sight of the whole mountain.

Philip knew this all too well. A successful businessman and Bible study leader in his church, he hadn't told anyone of his secret sexual sin. He'd been plagued with a porn addiction for thirteen years, so he'd lost hope. It was easier for him to fake it than to expose his secret. He assumed his addiction would dominate him for the rest of his days. He was so bogged down in his sin and shame that he couldn't see the wider landscape of God's plan for his life. Sometimes a bit of perspective can do a world of good.

When a struggler is so overwhelmed with his sin that he has lost perspective, it is good to step back and talk about the process of sanctification and the struggler's overall progress. For example, after I (Deepak) had been meeting with Philip for a few months, we had made significant progress. Philip had gone from looking at porn several times a day to looking at it once a week. The sin was not eradicated (yet), but we were moving in the right direction. But whenever Philip came in to talk, he was disappointed and skeptical, especially right after a fall. It wasn't unusual for him to take a distorted perspective of his sin struggles, bellowing comments like "This is never going to change!" or "What's the point? I've tried, and it doesn't seem to work. I'm going to be hooked for the rest of my life."

Really? I looked at Philip and commented, "Let's pull back the lens and get a wider view of your life. Recall for me where you were three months ago when we started meeting. How bad was it?"

Philip grimaced. "I was out of control. I was looking multiple times a day." Discouragement flashed in neon colors above his head.

"What about the last two weeks?"

Reluctantly, Philip said, "Last night was the first time I fell in fourteen days."

"Can't you see how far God has taken you?" I responded. "You have looked only once in the last fourteen days. Our goal is holiness and no sexual sin at all, but *you're headed in the right direction.* Look at how far God has already taken you."

You might think that my last comment was overblown enthusiasm, but it wasn't. I wanted Philip to step back and see what God was doing. It's so easy to get bogged down in the weeds and lose sight of God's glorious California mountain range.

The next time your friend is discouraged, if you can see progress and she can't, pull the lens back and help her to look at the bigger picture of God's work in her life. Give her a wide-angle view of the battle.

HOW CAN DISCIPLERS HELP STRUGGLERS TO SEE THE BIG PICTURE?

Your job as a discipler and helper is to be hopeful for the hopeless and to lend courage when they want to give up. Take these three big-picture perspectives and use them when you see that your friend is discouraged. Practically speaking, that might mean doing the following:

- Using the texts of Genesis 50:20, Romans 8:28, and James 1:2–4 to help the struggler to know that God uses even his foolishness for his good and to make him more like Christ.
- Using 1 John 3 to help the struggler to see how the final redemption offers perspective on where we are all headed. Do you have an example from your own life of how knowing the end of the story has helped you to persevere in your faith? If so, can you share it with the struggler?

- Highlighting any progress your friend has made in fighting sexual sin. Think of how God has worked in her in the past month, the past year, or maybe even the past few years. The perspective given by these time frames may lend encouragement to the struggler. It will help her to remember her plight when she first sought your assistance and to compare it to how things are right now.

Are you tempted to get discouraged and give up? Does it seem like the struggler you are helping is losing the battle with sexual sin? God is up to something in his life, and you have a front-row seat. Read these words from David Powlison, and let them fill your heart: "Christ comes with mercy for people who know their sins. His mercy leads to doing simple things that consistently head in the right direction. Do you feel discouraged and defeated by your struggle? Don't let anyone kid you that there's some magic answer and somehow you missed it. There are no magic answers. But a Person full of light is willing to walk with you in the direction of the light. He is willing to walk with you the whole way home."[3]

Porn strugglers often don't understand or see what God is doing. But as we come alongside them as disciplers, we should persevere with hope and trust (see Prov. 3:5–6), knowing that Christ hasn't given up.

Reflect: Do you see God working? Do you see progress in your friend's life? Have you seen change over the course of the last few months or years? If your answer is yes to any of these questions, take it upon yourself to help your friend to see it.

Act: Make it a regular habit (maybe once every few months) to step back and gauge your friend's progress and the bigger picture of what God is doing in her life.

21

ACKNOWLEDGING TRUE BEAUTY

*Have you ever watched a pornographic video
that emphasized beautiful character?*
—Tim Challies, *"Imperishable Beauty"*

*Do not let your adorning be external—the braiding of hair and the
putting on of gold jewelry, or the clothing you wear—but let your
adorning be the hidden person of the heart with the imperishable beauty
of a gentle and quiet spirit, which in God's sight is very precious.*
—1 Peter 3:3–4

Jamal has been viewing pornography since his youth. He first remembers being exposed to porn by his older brother around the age of five. That moment ignited a curiosity in Jamal's heart that he found difficult to understand and manage. Now, at age twenty-two, Jamal finds himself using pornography frequently. He battles intense guilt, knowing he has a hidden life.

Jamal has had numerous conversations with mentors in his small group, youth group leaders, and other men. But one element of counsel has been left out—how his view of what is truly beautiful and wholesome has been warped by pornography. When I (Jonathan) brought up this topic, Jamal showed a great deal of confusion. He knew his lust had very few boundaries. Porn was rampant in his life, and it spilled over into his interactions with women. Every physically attractive woman was a potential object of his lust. As does the typical porn struggler, Jamal dehumanized woman, reducing the women around him to mere objects of his lust and selfishness.

Jamal knew his view of women was distorted by his habitual use of pornography. He felt guilt over these distortions. He just didn't know what to do about it. Consequently, some days he tried desperately to suppress any feelings of attraction because he was afraid of his out-of-control lust. Other days, he gave in to his lust and was flirtatious. This all led to awkwardness with the women he knew at church. His experiences with pornography had confused his understanding of true beauty.

Author Alan Noble writes,

> It may be one of the hardest lessons that I have had to learn, that nearly all my purity efforts were built around denying and even condemning the beauty that God has created. . . . There are powerful forces in our culture and flesh driving us to view one another as bodies to be owned and captured. And unfortunately, there are also powerful forces in . . . our own hearts driving us to condemn and resent beauty. The church does well to fight against the abusive vision of sexuality promoted and profited off of by the world. . . . But we also need a richer theology of beauty and bodies.[1]

We need more than a *porn is wrong and bad for you* message to dissuade and persuade errant members of the church. No, a more godly perspective on beauty must be reclaimed. Our goal in this chapter is to think about how to help a believer like Jamal to embrace true beauty and reform the distortions of beauty created by the damage of pornography. We'll start by defining what beauty is and is not and then consider how to reform Jamal's perspective.

WHAT IS TRUE BEAUTY?

The world will offer you all kinds of definitions of beauty. How, as Christians, should we define and describe beauty? We'll start with this premise: to find out what is truly beautiful, we need to understand God's perspective on beauty.

True Beauty Starts with God

God is the standard for everything that's excellent. A quick scan of Scripture reveals that beauty appears all throughout its pages.

Out of Zion, the perfection of beauty,
God shines forth. (Ps. 50:2)

Splendor and majesty are before him;
strength and beauty are in his sanctuary. (Ps. 96:6)

He has made everything beautiful in its time. (Eccl. 3:11)

The Holy One of Israel
. . . has made you beautiful. (Isa. 60:9)

You shall be a crown of beauty in the hand of the Lord,
and a royal diadem in the hand of your God. (Isa. 62:3)

Even in places where the word *beauty* itself is not used, it is clear there is a beauty and purposefulness to God's created order. From the garden of Eden to the tabernacle, beauty is present. Moses records how even the garments of the priests were made with beauty in mind: "For Aaron's sons you shall make coats and sashes and caps. You shall make them for glory and beauty" (Ex. 28:40). Leland Ryken writes, "We need only use our senses to know that God created a world that is beautiful as well as functional. From a purely utilitarian point of view, God did not have to make a world filled with beautiful colors and symmetrical forms and varied textures and harmonious sounds. What we find here is not only a functional mind at work but also an artistic imagination. . . . The Christian doctrine of creation, therefore, affirms as good the artistic concern of both the creative artist and the audience with form, beauty, and artistry."[2]

God could have created a utilitarian, monochromatic, unimaginative world. Because we can see that what comes from God is beautiful, we know that beauty must be a part of his nature and character.

215

Ryken notes that beauty is not only integral to God's creative process but also a part of his character. There is not just "a functional mind at work but also an artistic imagination."

True Beauty May Be Physical

God-given beauty may be physical. A man or a woman sees someone of the opposite sex and recognizes them as physically attractive (see Song 1:15–16; 4:1–10). The lines and curves of the body, facial features, eye color, hair, physical stature—all these things add up to make one person attractive to another.

True Beauty May Be Spiritual

In the kingdom of God, beauty is more than skin-deep. God-given beauty is also spiritual. After all, God himself is spirit (see John 4:24), and he does not have a physical body. He is *the* standard for everything that is right, loving, good, holy, and true. All the non-visible, spiritual attributes come to their best and most excellent and perfect form in God himself.

While the Bible does commend a married couple's physical attraction to each other, it puts a greater emphasis on the beauty of a person's *character* and *heart* (see 1 Sam. 16:7; Prov. 31:30; 1 Peter 3:3–4). Is a person humble or arrogant, servant-hearted or selfish, patient or impatient, loving or greedy? We could go on with a list of noble attributes, but our point is best summed up with the question "Is this person Christlike?" The more a person lives like Christ and takes on his character, the more he or she is spiritually (not just physically) beautiful.

PORNOGRAPHY DISTORTS OUR SENSE OF TRUE BEAUTY

Jamal pursued, exploited, and consumed pornography's counterfeit beauty. Pornography lures us in with a fake beauty that is plastic, make-believe, fragmented, and disembodied.

Plastic. Many times, a man's or woman's beauty in a pornographic image or video is not his or her natural, God-given beauty. Rather, it's manipulated for the carnal pleasures of the porn consumer—with medical procedures or a mix of technologically fabricated pixels presented through a piece of hardware.

Make-believe. Sex ought to be an act of intimate love between a man and woman who are committed to each other in marriage. Pornography manufactures pretend scenarios for the self-indulgent satisfaction of our lusts.

Fragmented. The porn industry offers only the physical, lustful parts of "sex," without any relationship between the people involved or any knowledge of who they are. It's simply the act of sex on a camera.

Disembodied. Pornography users interact with people who exist on a screen. They are not even in the same place as the objects of their lust.

Pornography's fake beauty is an imitation and counterfeit of God's true beauty. Even if it were to drop the first category (plastic), it takes legitimate beauty and uses it in the wrong way—for the exploitation of bodies and for the consumption of sex, devoid of loving, trusting marital relationships.

After years of porn use, all Jamal knew were distortions and shallow imitations of true beauty. Women were physically attractive to him, and he lusted after them and fantasized about sexual interactions with them. But Jamal had no holistic sense that a woman could be beautiful for *both* her physical qualities and her Christlike character. His pornography addiction reduced his world to the size of his lusts. Any appreciation for beauty rooted in character or godliness was gone. It had been stripped away by his porn habit. Pornography addictions create consumers and purveyors rather than sacrificial lovers and servants. They consume image bearers for their own personal pleasure with no thought to who they are in real life.

Repeated interactions with pornography damage believers' minds and consciences. When it comes to their conception of beauty, all that matters are surgically remade faces and thighs and computer-adjusted images. Matthew Lee Anderson writes, "The normalization of unreasonable standards of beauty undermines men's satisfaction with their spouses while simultaneously makes meeting that standard a full-time job for women."[3] Porn also warps women's understanding of male attractiveness. How can husbands and wives, boyfriends and girlfriends, live up to the ridiculous standards created by the porn industry? They can't, and they shouldn't.

HOW DO WE GROW A STRUGGLER'S UNDERSTANDING OF TRUE BEAUTY?

How do we help Jamal to change his perspective on beauty? How can disciplers help those who are mired in pornography's fake beauty? We offer several suggestions.

Get Rid of Porn—the Distorter

Porn is the great distorter. We can't recover any sense of true beauty so long as it sticks around. Because Jamal's porn addiction has been the source of his troubles, we help him to begin to recover a true sense of beauty by getting porn out of his life. Everything we said in this book about fighting porn addictions comes into play here—cutting off access points, building solid accountability, connecting with gospel community, working to uncover heart issues, and so on. A life of purity and holiness is a perfect platform for recovering a biblical perspective on beauty.

Jamal worked to get pornography out of his life. But he also knew he had work to do in his heart and mind—a complete overhaul of his understanding of beauty—before he'd be ready to date or get married. That takes us to our next suggestion.

Grow the Struggler's Self-Awareness

When Scott (the discipler) and I (Jonathan) started helping Jamal, we didn't want to assume he understood the extent to which porn had distorted his perspective on beauty. We started by simply talking together about the distortions. We asked,

- What is true beauty? How would you define it? What's God's perspective?
- What's the world's perspective on beauty? What does the porn industry offer you? In what ways does pornography offer you a cheap imitation of true beauty?
- What does the character of God teach you about beauty? Is God himself beautiful? If so, in what way? If texts like Psalm 27:4 teach us to admire the Lord's beauty, what might that look like for you?
- How does your understanding of God, your love for Christ, and your faith in him change your perspective on beauty?

As we talked through these things, we were patient with Jamal. His redemption was the work not of one conversation, but of many conversations over many months. With patience and love, we witnessed firsthand how God peeled back the scales from his eyes to help him to see the distortions. Once he saw them, he could reject them.

Reject the Counterfeits

If a discipler recognizes that his friend has accepted porn's distortions and fake beauty, it's his responsibility to call this out. And if his friend, through the conviction of the Holy Spirit, comes to recognize that he's been embracing porn's faulty standards of beauty, he must repent of his wrong. Jamal's mentor, Scott, challenged him to reject the counterfeits and to pray for the Spirit to redeem the damage created by Jamal's habitual porn use.

The *Washington Post* ran the story of a man whose wife hired a photographer to take some racy photos of her and airbrush out her flaws. She obviously didn't feel like she could compete with the salacious images that our pornographic, sexually crazed culture holds out as examples of beauty. After looking at the photos she'd given him, the husband wrote the photographer a letter that makes our point beautifully:

When I opened the album that she gave to me, my heart sank. These pictures . . . are not my wife. [By making] every one of her "flaws" disappear . . . [you] took away everything that makes up our life. When you took away her stretch marks, you took away the documentation of my children. When you took away her wrinkles, you took away over two decades of our laughter, and our worries. When you took away her cellulite, you took away her love of baking and all the goodies we have eaten over the years. . . . Seeing these images made me realize that I honestly do not tell my wife enough how much I LOVE her and adore her just as she is. She hears it so seldom, that she actually thought these photoshopped images are what I wanted and needed her to look like. I have to do better, and for the rest of my days I am going to celebrate her in all her imperfectness. Thanks for the reminder.[4]

Our culture screams at us with ridiculous standards that form the foundation of our understanding of what is beautiful and attractive and worthy of our attention. The wife was deceived into thinking that this was what her husband wanted. Fortunately, she had a husband who rejected these worldly standards and the photographer's counterfeit photos.

When a Christian man and woman join together in marriage, physical and spiritual beauty both matter. But, as time progresses and the years add up, bodies change. Hair is lost; weight is gained; stretch marks and wrinkles appear. If Scripture is right—if character matters more than physical beauty—then what matters most (character) will grow over time as these believers become more spiritually mature. And what we'll find is that *spiritual maturity leads to greater spiritual beauty*.

What matters less (physical attractiveness) should not cause a person to second-guess her physical attraction to her spouse as his body changes over time. A mature perspective on physical beauty will not see a spouse's body's changes as liabilities but rather as markers of good and hard things that a husband and wife have experienced together over the years. *Spiritual maturity leads to a rejection of worldly standards of beauty, like the counterfeits and fake beauty that porn offers.* The mature embrace the physical changes that naturally come to their spouses, and they don't waver on their commitments.

Restore a Sense of Personhood to Image Bearers

The men and women depicted in porn are real human beings, even if they are conveyed through pixels on a screen. If someone confesses to looking at porn, you might say something like, "The woman you watched is someone who is made in the image of God. She has hopes and dreams and childhood memories, and she eats breakfast in the morning, just like you. She's a person." You might add, "That's someone's daughter you're looking at. How do you think her parents feel right now about what you're doing? How much do you think their hearts weep over this?"

The point is not to provoke shame or guilt. The point is to draw attention to how messed up this whole thing is—the porn user is staring at an image bearer whose life has been sacrificed on the altar of sex and money and exploitation to fulfill his self-gratification. We help the struggler to take a small step in the direction of a sense of true beauty by restoring his sense of the personhood of the people on the screen.

Acknowledge True Beauty

It is said that a good way to recognize counterfeit money is to know the characteristics of real money. In the same way, we better recognize the distortions that porn creates by coming to know what true beauty is. What we've seen is that true beauty starts with God. So for Jamal to get to know true beauty, he must come to behold and love God himself through his Son Jesus Christ. He must come to know God's character and grow to more closely resemble that character (see Eph. 5:1). Indeed, Jamal's (and our) purpose in life is to pursue the Lord's beauty. David writes,

> One thing have I asked of the LORD,
> that will I seek after:
> that I may dwell in the house of the LORD
> all the days of my life,
> to gaze upon the beauty of the LORD
> and to inquire in his temple. (Ps. 27:4)

The one thing David is set on pursuing is not riches, or adventure, or greater fame; it is dwelling with the Lord, the Beautiful One! Isn't it fascinating that a believer's pursuit of the Lord could be summarized as the pursuit of the Lord's beauty?

Love for Christ and his beauty changes our perspective on beauty in people. Therefore, the answer to habitual pornography is not asceticism from any and all beauty and attraction. Because each one of us is created in God's image, we too have the desire for beautiful things and the capacity to be beautiful and to create beautiful things.

We want Jamal to see life, the world, and other people through God's eyes. We could do this by looking at pictures of God's beautiful creation. But it's much more important for us to talk about God's attributes (to see God's beauty) and to think about beauty in other people (as Scripture commends; see, for example, Prov. 31:30). We could ask,

- What was the last beautiful thing you saw? How did you feel when you saw it? Why?
- Have you met anyone who's both physically beautiful and beautiful in his or her character? What was he or she like? What made him or her appealing to you?
- How might you grow in acknowledging and appreciating God's beauty? Have you ever grown in your knowledge and appreciation of his attributes?

As we talk with Jamal, we know that the Lord will work to rearrange and repair Jamal's understanding of biblical beauty! Having gotten rid of the distorted standards of porn's fake beauty and having embraced the true beauty found in God himself, he has room in his heart and mind to adopt God's perspective on beauty. God can help him to own and adopt new standards of beauty that look radically different from what world holds out as beauty. When we fall in love with Christ, he changes the way we view other people. Now *both* physical and spiritual beauty matter.

God, the great Creator, has made people beautiful (even in a sexual sense!). And his work in this area should not be dragged down by our lusts. Through the work of the Spirit in Jamal's heart, the help of his discipler, Scott, and repentance and faith, Jamal can come to own true beauty—the beauty that starts in God and spills over to the people he has made. He can appreciate the beauty of both character and physical attributes; beauty of servant-heartedness and also a smile; beauty of patience and also a shapely figure; beauty of trustworthiness and also an athletic frame. The reductionistic viewpoint of porn and lust no longer controls the way Jamal sees the world. Now God has expanded his sight so he can see both physical and spiritual beauty alike. Jamal sees true beauty in the people around him, and he is no longer enslaved to the faulty standards and dehumanizing effects of habitual porn.

Pray

The work of changing Jamal's perspective on beauty must ultimately be a work of the Spirit. Disciplers should ask questions about beauty to grow Jamal's self-awareness, press on Jamal's sense that the people on a screen are image bearers, and study the attributes of God, but the most important thing Scott and I (Jonathan) can do is to pray for God to change Jamal's heart.

Reflect: Before you help a friend like Jamal, take some time to think about your own views on beauty. In what ways has your own perception been distorted? How does it line up with that God values?

Act: Work through the questions above with your struggling friend. Take as much time as you need to establish what God values.

22

FIGHTING BATTLE WEARINESS

What sustained him for ups and downs of the long walk? . . .
He could daily seek Christ's mercies for what he needed that day:
forgiveness from the Lamb, strength from the King, protection in
the Refuge, guidance under the Shepherd's hand.
—David Powlison, "An Open Letter to Those
Debilitated by Their Sexual Sin"

And let us not grow weary of doing good,
for in due season we will reap, if we do not give up.
—Galatians 6:9

"I'm done."

Cynthia just couldn't keep going. She'd used Covenant Eyes, read her Bible, met with accountability, prayed often, gone to church, and listened to sermons, but, after several years, she was still struggling. No one had to convince her that what she was doing was wrong. She knew it. But that's not what brought on her *I-give-up* attitude.

Cynthia was weary. She was worn out from the daily battle— what felt like a never-ending fight to defeat her sexual sin. Cynthia was exhausted, discouraged, fatigued, despairing, and often hopeless.

A brand-new soldier arrives at the battlefront energized, carefully trained, sober-minded, vigilant, and ready for a fight. But after years of fighting, sometimes under hopeless circumstances, a battle weariness settles in and changes the attitude of the soldier. He moves from an initial *I-can-face-anything* attitude to *I can't do this anymore.* The soldier's mindset adopts a posture of hopelessness. Battle fatigue has taken over. He's ready to give up.

When Cynthia initially came to us for help, she was energized, humble, and eager to do the work. But as her sexual sin persisted over months, battle weariness settled in. She is not an exception. Sexual sin that persists over the long haul wears a struggler down, robbing her of joy and piling on disappointment, confusion, and self-loathing.

Is the person you are helping weary? Does he resemble a veteran in war, with battle fatigue setting in? The goal of this chapter is to help you to think about how to care for a believer who is exhausted from the fight with his sexual sin. What kind of hope can we lend to the hopeless? What can we do to help him to persevere in the fight against his sin?

HOW TO HELP A STRUGGLER TO PERSEVERE

We offer five suggestions on how a discipler can come alongside a battle-weary struggler.

Close the Gap between Sin and Repentance

There is often a delay between pornography strugglers' giving in to their sin and running to God in repentance. Shame, hopelessness, temporary despair, confusion, self-pity, and self-hatred all set in and slow a struggler from running to God. A struggler wants to do a little bit of self-atoning after he sins. He doesn't *really* believe that God will forgive him (contrary to 1 John 1:9), so he tries to clean himself up before he runs to Christ.

Strugglers grow weary in the battle with sin when they expend their energy on self-atoning exercises to absolve them of their sins rather than *running* to God in repentance and faith. Tony often does this—he will spend days being hard on himself (saying things like "I'm an idiot") before he confesses to his discipler.

As a discipler, you want to challenge a struggler who tends to expend his energy on self-atoning exercises. Remind Tony of Christ's sufficient atonement and plead with him to give up his habit of cleaning up his life *before* he comes to God. Self-atonement, self-pity, and self-condemnation all seem to run together. Exhort him to move quickly to repentance, trusting that God will forgive the penitent. Plead with him to believe and trust the promise of the gospel that God does forgive repentant sinners (see Luke 15) and offers them hope in the shadow of the cross.

"It seems counterintuitive to sin and then immediately to fall on your knees and say, 'God, be merciful to me, a sinner.' We harbor in our hearts the false belief that, somehow, we have to pay for our sins—just a little.

"But repentance isn't groveling. You repent when you agree with God that your sin is wicked and flee to the only one who can do helpless sinners any good. So, what if after you've sinned you didn't grovel for a week, but instead ran immediately to the Savior who 'came into the world to save sinners'?" **—David Sunday**[1]

Offer Loads and Loads of Encouragement

David Powlison would talk about the pervasive nature of our sin and brokenness as darkness enveloping us in a room. This room feels incredibly dark and hopeless, but imagine the difference a small three-watt nightlight would make. On its own, a three-watt nightlight might not seem like much, but in complete darkness it can provide immense hope and allow sight.

For the pornography struggler who is tempted to view her entire situation as hopeless, even small encouragement—the three-watt nightlight—makes a difference. If a three-watt light helps, imagine what a ten-thousand-watt light would do! Don't underestimate what your encouragement will do for a weary soul. Be deliberate in adding tons and tons of encouragement to your conversations, even when things are hard.

Let's say that Cynthia comes in and confesses to you that she's continuing to look at porn and hasn't had any success in fighting her sin this past week. Just the fact that she's showed up for help is a sign of God's grace in her life. She could have stayed home and wallowed in self-pity and self-condemnation. She could have hidden from you. *But she didn't.* She came back for help. If a struggler seems to be losing the battle more than winning but still keeps showing up for help, highlight that for her. "You look discouraged today, Cynthia. But your humility to keep coming back for help is an encouragement to me." And because you know God shows grace to the humble, point that out to her. "God shows grace—unmerited favor—to the humble. That's you. God hasn't given up on you, and so I won't either."

Here are a few other questions to help you to think about God's work in the struggler's life: In what ways are the struggler's responses to temptation slowly changing? When have you heard her speaking about her sin and brokenness in open and honest ways? Is she turning to God more quickly? Where do you see God's work in her life? Even if her progress is small, have you encouraged her? You'll be surprised at the difference a little encouragement can make in the life of someone who is weary.

Help a Struggler to Take a Renewed Look at How to Fight Sin

Sometimes a struggler like Tony has traveled so far and long with his sexual sin that he has lost perspective on how to keep fighting. As hopelessness and discouragement take over, he gives up. When battle weariness sets in, it helps a struggler to get a fresh perspective.

This is when it helps to fight a problem in community rather than in isolation. God meant for strugglers to lock arms with stronger, more mature believers who can help to carry them along on their most weary days. Encourage an exhausted Tony to get feedback from those around him. For example, consider the following:

- Problems don't stay static but change over time. Examine whether Tony has new triggers or has been caught up in difficult new circumstances. Are triggers going undetected and thus failing to be prevented in a way that holds Tony back?
- Drawing up new accountability measures helps to recommit the struggler to the process. Has the accountability become

less vulnerable, less honest, less vigilant, less grace-centered, less Word-driven, or less hopeful? Talk about what needs to be changed and what should happen in the days ahead.

- In a culture in which relationships are often temporary, and there is a good bit of churn and turnover among friends, have those in Tony's inner circle of relationships moved on to other seasons of life or other parts of the country or other churches? Sometimes it can revitalize the struggler to have new allies come alongside him. They can give him fresh incentive to fight.

- Sometimes the common means of grace need to be embraced with renewed vigor. Tony has slacked off or become inconsistent in reading the Bible, praying, attending church, and participating in his small group and other forms of Christian fellowship. His discpler (Fred) can talk through a realistic Bible reading plan with him; he can encourage Tony to give a phone call to his small-group leader; he can save a seat for Tony at the Sunday worship service so they can sit together as Tony recommits to be at church.

What other areas need to be readdressed and strengthened? Who can Tony talk to in order to rethink how he's addressing his sin? What we're looking for is a new perspective, because a new perspective can provide the weary struggler with a renewed hope in fighting against sin and a new sense of potential progress.

Draw the Struggler Back to the Cross

Persistent sexual sin wears Cynthia down, robbing her of joy and piling on disappointment. When she is at this point, we ought to point her to Christ for strength. Sadly, though, we are tempted to look for something novel or some new approach to aid her. Ask yourself the following questions:

- *Do you really believe the gospel is enough?* Pause, don't rush by that question.

- *Do you see Christ as essential to defeating sexual sin?* Again, slow down and answer this question before you move on. A new technique, method, or strategy isn't enough. Christ is.

When a porn struggler is tired, you don't need something new as much as something old—so point her to the good news Christ brings.

The author of Hebrews does a marvelous job of connecting Christ to our propensity to grow tired and weary:

> Therefore, since we are surrounded by so great a cloud of witnesses, let us also lay aside every weight, and sin which clings so closely, and let us run with endurance the race that is set before us, looking to Jesus, the founder and perfecter of our faith, who for the joy that was set before him endured the cross, despising the shame, and is seated at the right hand of the throne of God. *Consider him who endured from sinners such hostility against himself, so that you may not grow weary or fainthearted.* (Heb. 12:1–3)

Having examined the persevering saints in the previous chapter of his book, the author of Hebrews now says, "As we keep our eyes on the enduring faith of all these witnesses, let's now talk about *you.*" His exhortation is twofold: (1) "lay aside every weight, and sin which clings so closely" and (2) "let us run with endurance the race that is set before us." But the key comes in the next phrase: "looking to Jesus." Christ endured the cross; he endured hostility from sinners; he endured God's wrath for our sin; he endured all this *for us.* So the exhortation in verse 3 is "Consider him." It is by keeping our eyes fixed on Jesus that the weary and fainthearted receive strength.

What do you talk about in your conversations? The worst kind of help is Christless. Give us five minutes, and we can spit out advice. Much of it will sound pretty good. But is it Christ-centered? As disciplers and friends, does what we say take our struggling friends back to the only One who can make a true difference? Do we show them the glories of Calvary?

You will be tempted to get tired of talking about the gospel. But you must not stop. You must tell the porn struggler about Jesus . . . *repeatedly*. Once is never enough. Christ is the struggler's only true hope for winning the battle against sexual sin over the long haul. Only by believing in Christ, and fighting to believe again the next day, and fighting to believe again the next day, do strugglers endure in the fight.

Every time a struggler comes back to us with a battle-weary mentality, we respond, "Consider him." It's because Christ provides supernatural strength for this fight (see Eph. 3:16) and his grace helps us to say no to ungodliness and passions and to live self-controlled and upright lives (see Titus 2:11–13) that weary strugglers like Tony and Cynthia can endure to the end.

Ground the Struggler in the Love of God in Christ

The love of God should be the struggler's primary motivation for change and growth. When religious opponents argued with John Bunyan in prison, they urged him not to assure his Christian friends of God's unswerving love. "If you keep assuring the people of God's love," the opponents argued, "they will do whatever they want." Bunyan replied, "If I assure God's people of his love, then they will do whatever he wants."[2]

Love transforms people. When strugglers grow confident in God's love, they grow confident in what God asks of them. They are more inclined to fight sin and less willing to listen to the world; they feel more known and accepted by God and more willing to make sacrifices for him. We then want to do everything we can to remind strugglers of the love God demonstrated for them through his Son's death on the cross. God's love through Christ is the clearest and most pronounced display of the Father's love in all of history (see Rom. 5:8).

HOW TO HELP YOURSELF TO PERSEVERE

There's one other person's weariness to address—yours! Yes, there are days when *you*, the discipler, will want to throw in the towel.

The work is hard. Progress is two steps forward, one step back, and a half step forward. Frustrating, isn't it? There will be opportunities for discouragement, confusion, anger, and disbelief. You will want to draw back and give up. What do you do?

Remember Who the Change Agent Is

When the struggler's battle seems to be moving at a glacial pace, remember that it is God, working through his Spirit and his Word, who accomplishes change in someone's life. That helpfully takes the pressure off you and puts it in the right place. God must work. If he doesn't, nothing will significantly change. We know God's promises, so we can feel assured that he will work in these hard situations, even if we don't see much fruit from our work. God has promised he will change his children and transform them to be like his Son (see Rom. 8:29), and we can rest assured in that promise.

Take People as They Are, Not as You Want Them to Be

It's far too easy to focus on what someone *should be* rather than deal with the hurting or confused person standing right in front of you. Listen, ask questions, be present with the weary person, and pay close attention to how his long-term plight is affecting his heart right now.

Look to God for Strength

Weariness is a common experience for disciplers. As we come alongside strugglers who don't make much progress, who reject our advice, who are inconsistent in following our guidance, there comes a point at which every discipler starts to think, "I'm tired. I'm not sure if I should keep going."

Consider David's cry in Psalm 6:

O LORD, rebuke me not in your anger,
    nor discipline me in your wrath.
Be gracious to me, O LORD, for I am languishing;
    heal me, O LORD, for my bones are troubled.

My soul also is greatly troubled.
    But you, O LORD—how long?
Turn, O LORD, deliver my life;
    save me for the sake of your steadfast love.
For in death there is no remembrance of you;
    in Sheol who will give you praise?

I am weary with my moaning;
    every night I flood my bed with tears;
    I drench my couch with my weeping.
My eye wastes away because of grief;
    it grows weak because of all my foes. (vv. 1–7)

We're not certain about David's situation in Psalm 6—he may have been fighting his sin or some kind of sickness. He may have been in the middle of a crisis or fending off his enemies. But what we do know for sure is that he was "languishing" (v. 2), "weary" with moaning (v. 6), and weeping every night (v. 6). He was exhausted.

What did David do? Psalm 6 records that he looked to the Lord as the source of his strength. "Be gracious to me, O LORD" (v. 2). "Turn, O LORD, deliver my life" (v. 4). He expressed his confidence in the Lord's steadfast love and the fact that the Lord would hear his pleas for help.

What a wonderful example David is for all of us, regardless of our circumstances. If we're exhausted as disciplers, we can look to the Lord and have confidence in him when we are weary. (That's good news for many of us who walk around exhausted by life's troubles!)

In fact, unlike us, God *never* grows weary or tired. The prophet Isaiah tells us, "The LORD is the everlasting God, the Creator of the ends of the earth. He does not faint or grow weary; his understanding is unsearchable" (Isa. 40:28). And that brings us to even more good news! The everlasting God strengthens those who trust in him:

He gives power to the faint,
    and to him who has no might he increases strength.

233

Even youths shall faint and be weary,
   and young men shall fall exhausted;
but they who wait for the Lord shall renew their strength;
   they shall mount up with wings like eagles;
   they shall run and not be weary;
   they shall walk and not faint. (Isa. 40:29–31)

If you are exhausted, Isaiah's promise is that "they who wait for the Lord shall renew their strength." Does that encourage you? Are you looking to him for your strength? You need a source of strength to endure this battle, just like the struggler. God has not forgotten you.

Reflect: If your friend is weary, what do you need to do to encourage her faith and refocus her back on the cross?

Act: Offer a kind word. Pick one way you see the grace of God working in your friend's life and tell her about it.

CONCLUSION:
LOOKING FORWARD TO A BETTER DAY

HOW TO BECOME A MORE SKILLED DISCIPLER

Years ago, I (Deepak) started my amateur career as a baker. I attempted to cook all kinds of savory and sweet food for my family. *Attempt* is the key word in that last sentence, as my family endured countless burned meals and not-so-good desserts. My skills were lacking, and they didn't improve much. (Much to the dismay of my family.) Halfway through writing this book, I stumbled across an Instagram account with pictures of exquisite-looking meals. After I had spent a few moments scrolling through the pictures, it occurred to me that the account belonged to my coauthor Jonathan. It turns out he's a very gifted chef. Looking at the pictures of his meals was both inspiring and intimidating.

Maybe you've come to the end of this book and its twenty-two skills and are thinking, "I can't wait to get started!" We're glad for your enthusiasm, and we trust God will use you to do great things for him. Or maybe you're wondering, "Is this too much for me? I don't know if I can do this." You may think, "There are a lot of skills to master, and I'm just a novice." Like me, you want to be better at your craft. You see your amateur skills and how far you have to go, and you feel discouraged. What can you do? Go to any skilled worker—athlete, lawyer, chef, carpenter—and ask him or her what it took to grow his or her skills from *mediocre* to *top notch*.

Here's what we think you'll hear.

Learn One Skill at a Time

When I (Deepak) took golf lessons in high school, the instructor gave me about twenty things to remember as I swung my number two club at the ball. After the lesson, I stood next to the tee, trying to keep in mind the dozens of tips the instructor had offered. It was too much.

As you get started, don't attempt a dozen new skills at one time. Our recommendation is to pick one skill and focus on it for a while, until you're more comfortable with it. Then pick another. And another, and so on. Try to master a skill or two at a time and be patient as you grow your skills. Your discipling won't all change at once. It will take time to develop your skills.

Practice, Practice, Practice

Are you ready and willing to put in the hard work needed? Watch a chef or athlete grow in his skills. He practices a new technique not just once or twice but dozens of times. It's in the repetition of the skill—over and over and over again—that mastery comes.

So, for example, as you start to learn to ask questions, you may feel that you're just okay at the skill. Don't let that deter you. In every conversation you have, ask questions of the person near you to see if you can get him or her to open up and if you can gain access to his or her heart. With time and lots of practice, you'll get better at it.

Be Disciplined

Why will you keep practicing? Because you're disciplined. You're not lazy or inconsistent. You're committed to getting better, and this will be shown in your willingness to train and do the hard work. If you read this and think, "I'm not the disciplined type," then you may need to ask a friend for accountability as you work to grow in these skills.

Be Willing to Fail

Let's say you set out to listen more diligently and pursue people's hearts. In your first conversation with your struggling friend, you ask a few heart-oriented questions to get her to open up more. Maybe she's not very self-aware. Or maybe she's not used to being vulnerable so early on in the relationship. She resists your questions. From her superficial responses and her uncomfortable facial expressions, it's clear that she's not ready to have a heart-to-heart conversation. You fail to get her to be honest about her sin.

If you are not willing to fail, you will never learn to succeed. You will run into lots of situations as a discipler in which you won't succeed. But it is in the failing that you'll gain insight and get better at these skills.

TWO *D*'S TO LIVE BY

As you grow in your skills, you should also think about how your struggling friend grows in faith, maturity, and Christlikeness. We offer a few final words to you, the discipler, as we depart. Let's consider two *D*s—*direction* and *destination*.

Direction

When thinking about your friend's sanctification, we should always keep the direction in mind. David Powlison writes, "What matters most is not the distance you've covered. It's not the speed you're going. It's not how long you've been a Christian. It's the direction you're headed."[1] What is the direction in which your friend is headed? It is *toward* Christ. She daily sheds her sinful habits bit by bit and grows in Christlikeness.

We've endeavored to come back again and again to the gospel, because we know it has the power to change struggling sinners and help them to endure with true joy (see Col. 1:11). It is in a person's movement toward Christ—by the strength God provides for her, through her hope in God's promises, with the conviction of the Spirit, and through your humble guidance—that a life can be changed for the good.

Let's say your friend is headed toward Christ but strays off the path. You'll have frustrating and hard times—he falls and confesses so many times, you lose count; you hit moments when you don't know what to say anymore; you're disappointed in yourself (you don't think you're really helping); or your friend is apathetic about fighting his sin. It is your faith and hope in Christ that keeps you engaged, so that you can call out to your friend, "Stay on the path toward Christ!" Like Evangelist, who showed up when Christian wandered off the straight and narrow path in *The Pilgrim's Progress*, so you, with the Lord's help, will keep your friend headed in the right direction.

Say Jayne comes in to confess her sin to you. She's fallen a couple of times over the last month, but that's much better than six months ago, when she was looking at porn daily. She's weary and discouraged because she still occasionally falls prey to sexual sin. She starts crying. You look at her—her puffy eyes, tightened facial muscles, bleeding mascara. She's broken over her foolishness.

Yet she's headed in the right direction. Things are not perfect (and they never will be in this life!), but they are better than when you started working together. Consequently, you tell her, "You're discouraged that sin still hinders you. But know this, Jayne: you're headed in the right direction. I've been encouraged by your daily work, your faith, and your persistence. Let's keep going!"

You look at another biblical text—Isaiah 53. You utter a quick prayer and read the text out loud. She's struck not only by what Jesus did for her but by who he is and what he is like. She has a moment of genuine insight. You're delighted. You talk about Isaiah's Suffering Servant with her because you want to remind her of her direction— toward Christ.

You may not know what the next month holds, let alone the next year. But you know Jayne is a believer. You know that she's coming to you and in humility seeking help. You know that the Bible gives her hope because it points her in the right direction. Jayne struggles many days, but she doesn't let the hard days overwhelm her anymore. Because she knows she's headed in the right direction, she keeps going.

Destination

When fighting pornography, we not only keep the struggler headed in the right direction but keep her eyes set on the destination.

If the direction is *toward Christ,* the destination is *eternity with Christ in the new heaven and the new earth.*

Hollywood often deceives us into thinking that heaven is about cute little angels sitting on white clouds. What do you think heaven is about? Consider the testimony of the apostle John:

> Then I saw a new heaven and a new earth, for the first heaven and the first earth had passed away, and the sea was no more. And I saw the holy city, new Jerusalem, coming down out of heaven from God, prepared as a bride adorned for her husband. *And I heard a loud voice from the throne saying, "Behold, the dwelling place of God is with man. He will dwell with them, and they will be his people, and God himself will be with them as their God.* He will wipe away every tear from their eyes, and death shall be no more, neither shall there be mourning, nor crying, nor pain anymore, for the former things have passed away."
>
> And he who was seated on the throne said, "Behold, I am making all things new." Also he said, "Write this down, for these words are trustworthy and true." (Rev. 21:1–5)

Let's focus on verse 3 (italicized). What's the main idea here? God will dwell with mankind. At the end of time, the greatest blessing of heaven is that God's redeemed people—those who have repented of their sins and put their trust in Christ—will have unhindered fellowship with him for all eternity. The point is not that our struggling friends will be with cute angels or sitting on white clouds or standing in front of pearly gates. The point is their destination—the new heaven and new earth, where they'll be with God for all eternity.

Why does this matter? How does this destination have anything to do with today? If the struggler keeps his eyes set on the destination, it should affect how he lives *right now.* Let's say I record the Super Bowl because it's taking place during the evening service at our church. Despite my pleas to my children not to tell me the score, as soon as I walk in the door, my daughter tells me, "Tom Brady and the Tampa Bay Bucs beat the New Orleans Saints!" Because I know final score, that affects how I watch the recording of the game. Even if the Bucs fall behind, I won't worry because I know who wins in the end.

In the same way, if a struggler knows his destination, his failures in fighting sexual sin right now don't have to ruin him. He knows where he is headed, and he knows that God's steadfast love and faithfulness guarantee that he will safely make it there (see Phil. 1:6). That makes a difference in how the struggler lives right now. He can live with confidence that God will get him home.

Anytime I (Deepak) am driving and turn my head away from the road, my youngest son screams from the back of the van, "Keep your eyes on the road, Pops!" In the weariness of the battles, it's easy to get caught up with the bad things happening today and lose sight of where we are headed.

What does that look like in the day-to-day skirmishes against pornography? If Jayne falls to sin a couple times in a week, she gets overwhelmed and loses perspective. Her shame becomes so pronounced she feels dirty, rejected, and outside God's kingdom. She condemns herself and gives in to her discouragement. All these things take her eyes off her destination.

God has a destination set up in your friend's GPS. You, as the discipler, get to keep reminding him, "Keep your eyes on the destination!" Your friend's job is to trust the Lord and obey even on the hardest of days, for his faith will keep his eyes set on the destination.

Keep your friend's focus on where he's headed—to be with the Lord in glory. He will see Christ, seated at the right hand of God the Father, in all his glory, majesty, and might. At that moment, he'll know, beyond a shadow of a doubt, that the fight is finished and the war is finally won. No more battles to be waged. No more temptations. No more hard days. No more disappointments. No more struggles. No more sexual escapades. It's all gone.

Your struggling friend can take comfort right now that one day this messy life will be done with and we won't have to fight our sin anymore. Can you, as the disicpler, help your friend to see this destination? Can you help your friend to look forward to the day when sin will be gone?

In glory, your friend will know that he is free . . . forever. Are you looking forward to that day? Is your friend looking forward to that day? Glory be to God.

ACKNOWLEDGMENTS

FROM DEEPAK

I'm grateful to my family, who patiently waited on me while I churned out this book during the first part of my 2020 summer sabbatical. I'm especially grateful to my dear wife who has read through everything I've ever written. She kindly edited this book, so you (the reader) owe her a thank-you too.

I'm also grateful to the pastors of Capitol Hill Baptist Church. What a joy it is, brothers, to co-labor with you. I am grateful for the privilege of serving on staff for over a decade.

I'm also grateful to the congregation, who kindly recognize the need for pastors to have a break and get a sabbatical. The church expects me to work hard (and I do!), but they also recognize how often pastors burn out. So they give our staff breaks for the sake of rest and spiritual renewal. I'm confident that I've made it this far because of God's grace primarily, but secondarily because the congregation has afforded me time off. I'm confident this will help me to run the race over the long haul.

What I've also loved is watching our church be so outward-focused—from the numbers in our budget, to less glamorous overseas service (like childcare trips for missionaries), to hosting pastors all year round. Time and time again, I've been astounded at (and instructed by) how our church constantly works for the good of other pastors, churches, and missionaries.

Finally, I'm grateful for Jonathan. Brother, what a joy to see our friendship growing and to have now done two books together. The more I've gotten to know you, the more I've treasured God's work in you and through you. I didn't want this book to be just from my vantage point, so the readers have been much better served by your grace, love, and wisdom.

FROM JONATHAN

Writing acknowledgments to a book is both an impossible task and a task that brings much joy. Impossible because there is no way to acknowledge every person who has contributed to this process, and joyful because to recount individuals' help along the way brings about such pleasant memories and thankfulness.

First, thank you to my wife and family for bearing with me through this process. Many an evening, I would come home talking about this book and the challenges I was experiencing. They remained curious, prayerful, and interested throughout the journey, ever supportive. Jennifer, thank you for always offering whatever was needed to finish the book—whether I was taking time away or coming home late—and for bearing with my weariness at times! I love you all.

Second, thank you to many of you who read various edits and drafts of the chapters as we went along: Marsha Raymond, Joy King, Sue Moroney, Joel Harris, and Melissa Affolter.

Third, thank you to my counselees, many of whom read through various drafts and contributed helpful suggestions and even testimonials. This book is for you in so many ways. May God continue to give you the grace to persevere, and may you grow in your love for him each and every day in every way!

Finally, Deepak, a huge debt of gratitude is due you. You kindly brought me along on this project and every step of the way guided our writing. This book would not exist without your aid. You have been a deep encouragement to my soul. At times when I was unsure if we would reach the finish line, you spurred us on . . . refocused our gaze . . . and offered a clear picture of the end goal. You are a treasured friend and colleague.

FROM BOTH OF US

This book and writing was a community project. We drew on the wisdom and experience of a lot of friends, colleagues, and ministry partners.

Thanks to the P&R team for their patience as we wrote this book. It arrived long overdue. But you got two books, when you were only planning for one! Thanks to Dave Almack, Bryce Craig, and the entire staff.

Thank you especially to Amanda Martin and Aaron Gottier. Amanda and Aaron edited *Rescue Plan* and *Rescue Skills*, and through their tireless labors, godly counsel, thoughtful questions, and careful rewording of sentences, they helped us to make them better books. The first draft of these two books went to our endorsers. Because of Amanda and Aaron's work, we think the second draft is even better than what the endorsers read.

Editors are really the unsung heroes of the publishing world, doing Christ-honoring labor behind the scenes. If you ever meet Amanda or Aaron, do thank them. They've probably helped you more than you realize.

NOTES

Foundational Information from *Rescue Plan*
1. The first three *As* (*access*, *anonymity*, and *appetite*) were inspired by Heath Lambert's discussion of this subject.

Chapter 1: Listening with an Active Ear
1. See Adam S. McHugh, *The Listening Life: Embracing Attentiveness in a World of Distraction* (Downers Grove, IL: IVP Books, 2015), 18.
2. Tremper Longman III, *Proverbs*, Baker Commentary on the Old Testament Wisdom and Psalms (Grand Rapids: Baker Academic, 2006), 357.
3. McHugh, *The Listening Life*, 137–38.

Chapter 2: Targeting the Heart
1. G. K. Beale, *We Become What We Worship: A Biblical Theology of Idolatry* (Downers Grove, IL: IVP Academic, 2008); Michael R. Emlet, "Understanding the Influences on the Human Heart," *Journal of Biblical Counseling* 20, no. 2 (Winter 2002): 47–52; Elyse Fitzpatrick, *Idols of the Heart: Learning to Long for God Alone*, 2nd ed. (Phillipsburg, NJ: P&R Publishing, 2016); Timothy Keller, *Counterfeit Gods: The Empty Promises of Money, Sex, and Power, and the Only Hope That Matters* (2009; repr., New York: Penguin Books, 2011); Jeremy Pierre, *The Dynamic Heart in Daily Life: Connecting Christ to Human Experience* (Greensboro, NC: New Growth Press, 2016); David Powlison, "Idols of the Heart and 'Vanity Fair,'" *Journal of Biblical Counseling* 13, no. 2 (Winter 1995): 35–50; James K. A. Smith, *You Are What You Love: The Spiritual Power of Habit* (Grand Rapids: Brazos Press, 2016).
2. Emlet, "Understanding the Influences on the Human Heart," 47. Emphasis in original.

Chapter 3: Developing a Plan

1. We've adopted the word *public* from Edward T. Welch, *Addictions: A Banquet in the Grave* (Phillipsburg, NJ: P&R Publishing, 2001), 220–21.

2. This sentence is a paraphrase from the introduction Jeremy Pierre wrote to an unpublished manuscript (last updated March 26, 2013), Microsoft Word file. We're grateful for his help.

3. This section is adapted from Pierre's unpublished manuscript. The four fronts (God, self, others, circumstance) are a paradigm that Jeremy and I (Deepak) came up with for our book *The Pastor and Counseling: The Basics of Shepherding Members in Need* (Wheaton, IL: Crossway, 2015), and it is further elaborated in section 2 of Jeremy's book *The Dynamic Heart in Daily Life: Connecting Christ to Human Experience* (Greensboro, NC: New Growth Press, 2016).

Chapter 6: Asking the Right Questions

1. See Paul David Tripp, *Instruments in the Redeemer's Hands* (Phillipsburg, NJ: P&R Publishing, 2002), 168.

2. See Michael R. Emlet, *Cross Talk: Where Life and Scripture Meet* (Greensboro, NC: New Growth Press, 2009), 66.

Chapter 7: Becoming Accountability That Works

1. John Freeman, *Hide or Seek: When Men Get Real with God about Sex* (Greensboro, NC: New Growth Press, 2014), 78.

2. Some of these questions were adapted from Donald S. Whitney, *Ten Questions to Diagnose Your Spiritual Health* (Colorado Springs: NavPress, 2001).

3. Jason Hsieh provided this idea about ungracious accountability in an email message to Deepak Reju on May 29, 2017.

4. Thanks again to Jason Hsieh.

Chapter 9: Discerning Fake Repentance

1. See C. John Miller, *Repentance and 21st Century Man* (Fort Washington, PA: Christian Literature Crusade, 2003), 15, 17. This is a reprint of Miller's 1975 work *Repentance and 20th Century Man*.

2. Quoted in Richard J. Foster, *Celebration of Discipline: The Path to Spiritual Growth*, rev. ed. (San Francisco: HarperSanFrancisco, 1988), 143.

3. The topic of this section was inspired by Darby Strickland, "How to Discern True Repentance When Serious Sin Has Occurred," *Journal of Biblical Counseling*, 34, no. 3 (2020): 41.

4. Sinclair Ferguson, *The Grace of Repentance* (repr., Wheaton, IL: Crossway, 2010), 25, 39.

Chapter 10: Encouraging Genuine Repentance

1. See Paul Barnett, *The Second Epistle to the Corinthians*, The New International Commentary on the New Testament (Grand Rapids: William B. Eerdmans, 1997), 372–73.

2. "[The Corinthians'] grief was worked by God and rested in his hand." Mark A. Seifrid, *The Second Letter to the Corinthians*, The Pillar New Testament Commentary (Grand Rapids: William B. Eerdmans, 2014), 309. The literal translation of "godly grief" is a grief according to God or according to the will of God.

3. See homily 15.2, on 2 Corinthians 7:10, in John Chrysostom's *Homilies on Second Corinthians*, as well as David E. Garland, *2 Corinthians*, The New American Commentary 29 (Nashville: B&H Publishing Group, 1999), 356.

4. Because the relationship between the Corinthians and the apostle was strained, in this case repentance before Paul was the same thing as repentance before God. Titus reported to Paul that the Corinthians had turned back to Paul because he had rebuked them in his severe letter: "As he [Titus] told us of your longing, your mourning, your zeal *for me*, so that I rejoiced still more" (2 Cor. 7:7). So the repentance Paul describes took place on a very specific occasion between the Corinthians and the apostle, yet we know "the evidences of the Corinthians' repentance illustrate the marks which will appear in all true repentance." Sinclair Ferguson, *The Christian Life: A Doctrinal Introduction* (1981; repr., Carlisle, PA: Banner of Truth Trust, 2001), 76. For more on the relationship of the Corinthians, Paul, and the severe letter, see Barnett, *Second Epistle*, 377–78, and Seifrid, *Second Letter*, 310.

5. See John MacArthur, *The MacArthur Bible Commentary* (Nashville: Thomas Nelson, 2005), 1,636. To read about each of these characteristics in greater detail, see also Heath Lambert, "Using Sorrow to Fight Pornography," chap. 2 in *Finally Free: Fighting for Purity with the Power of Grace* (Grand Rapids: Zondervan, 2013), and Richard Owen Roberts, "Seven Marks of Repentance," chap. 6 in *Repentance: The First Word of the Gospel* (Wheaton, IL: Crossway, 2002).

6. See Lambert, *Finally Free*, 37.

7. Kelly Needham, "Repentance Is a Posture," The Gospel Coalition, September 21, 2017, https://www.thegospelcoalition.org/article/repentance-is-a-posture/. Emphasis in original.

8. Charles Hedman, email message to Deepak Reju, May 8, 2020.

9. Bryan Chapell, *Holiness by Grace: Delighting in the Joy That Is Our Strength* (Wheaton, IL: Crossway, 2001), 72.

10. Sinclair Ferguson, *The Grace of Repentance* (repr., Wheaton, IL: Crossway, 2010), 54.

11. Lambert, *Finally Free*, 26. Emphasis in original.

12. See Jennifer Greenberg, "8 Signs of True Repentance," The Gospel Coalition, October 4, 2019, https://www.thegospelcoalition.org/article/8-signs-true -repentance/.

13. Chapell, *Holiness by Grace*, 84.

14. Chapell, 90.

15. Psalm 51 is arranged in a chiastic structure, making verse 12 its center point. For a thorough exposition and analysis of Psalm 51, we recommend David Covington, "Psalm 51: Repenter's Guide," *Journal of Biblical Counseling* 20, no. 1 (Fall 2001): 21–39.

16. "Continual Repentance," in *The Valley of Vision: A Collection of Puritan Prayers and Devotions*, ed. Arthur Bennett (1975; repr., Carlisle, PA: Banner of Truth Trust, 2002), 76.

Chapter 11: Taking a Wider Gaze at Sin

1. David Powlison, "Sexual Sin and the Wider, Deeper Battle," *Journal of Biblical Counseling* 24, no. 2 (Spring 2006): 30. I (Deepak) got the idea of "The Problem" from David's article.

2. "Ministering to someone who is starting to battle a half-dozen foes that were previously invisible is extremely heartening!" Powlison, 33. See also p. 30.

3. "We can't draw a straight line from fear to anxiety or from anger to abuse. Instead, various struggles combine and build upon one another to produce one or more issues." Robert K. Cheong, *Restore: Changing How We Live and Love* (Greensboro, NC: New Growth Press, 2020), 21.

4. All three of these conditions—anxiety and stress; fantasy and control; sensuality and worldliness—we got from John Henderson, "The Pornography Ecosystem," in *Porn and the Pastor: The Life and Death Consequences of Addiction in Ministry*, ed. C. Jeffrey Robinson and Garrett Kell (Louisville: SBTS Press, 2018), 38–40.

5. Henderson, 38.

6. Although the examples under the fantasy and control category are of heterosexual fantasy, plenty of Christians struggle with homosexual fantasy but do

not act on those same-sex desires in order to remain faithful to Scripture's teaching on homosexuality.

7. This example is based on a story by David Powlison in *Making All Things New: Restoring Joy to the Sexually Broken* (Wheaton, IL: Crossway, 2017), 80–81.

8. See John Freeman, *Hide or Seek: When Men Get Real with God about Sex* (Greensboro, NC: New Growth Press, 2014), 109.

Chapter 12: Reviving a Dead Conscience

1. See Andrew David Naselli and J. D. Crowley, *Conscience: What It Is, How to Train It, and Loving Those Who Differ* (Wheaton, IL: Crossway, 2016), 22–23.

2. See Naselli and Crowley, 41.

3. See John MacArthur, *The Vanishing Conscience* (Dallas: Word, 1994), 39, referenced in Naselli and Crowley, 58.

4. See MacArthur, 44, referenced in Naselli and Crowley, 41.

5. See Naselli and Crowley, 70.

6. See Naselli and Crowley, 64.

7. See Naselli and Crowley, 65.

Chapter 13: Instilling Identity

1. Timothy Keller, *Making Sense of God: An Invitation to the Skeptical* (New York: Viking, 2016), 124.

2. See Rom. 15:15; 1 Cor. 4:17; 15:1; 2 Cor. 10:7; 2 Tim. 1:5–6; 2:14; Titus 3:1; Heb. 3:12–13; 2 Peter 1:13; 3:1; Jude 5.

Chapter 15: Overcoming Temptations

1. John Owen, "Of Temptation: The Nature and Power of It," in *Overcoming Sin and Temptation: Three Classic Works by John Owen*, ed. Kelly M. Kapic and Justin Taylor, redesigned ed. (Wheaton, IL: Crossway, 2015), 156.

2. See Ed Welch, "How to Slay the Dragon of Pornography," The Gospel Coalition, February 23, 2016, https://www.thegospelcoalition.org/article/how-to-slay-the-dragon-of-pornography/. Though the words in the section are ours, Ed's article prompted us to write about how the idea of boundaries connects to the redemptive story.

3. See Thomas Brooks, *Precious Remedies against Satan's Devices* (repr., Carlisle, PA: Banner of Truth Trust, 2011), 29.

4. C. S. Lewis, *The Screwtape Letters* (1942; repr., New York: HarperCollins, 2001), 44.

5. Joe Harrod, "Overcoming Temptation," The Gospel Coalition, April 7, 2020, https://www.thegospelcoalition.org/essay/overcoming-temptation/.

6. See Owen, "Of Temptation," 205. Owen writes, on that same page, "Watch, then, to understand betimes the snares that are laid for you—to understand the advantages your enemies have against you, before they get strength and power, before they are incorporated with your lusts, and have distilled poison into your soul."

7. See Owen, 192–94.

8. See Owen, 197–201.

9. See Owen, 201–2.

10. See Owen, 203.

12. See Owen, 194.

12. See Owen, 194.

13. See Owen, 196.

14. Owen, 204.

15. This sentence is a modernized restatement of Owen: "Lay in store of gospel provisions that may make the soul a defensed place against all the assaults thereof" (205).

16. See Owen, 204. He states, "When men can live and plod on in their profession, and not be able to say when they had any living sense of the love of God or of the privileges which we have in the blood of Christ, I know not what they can have to keep them from falling into snares. The apostle tells us that the 'peace of God shall keep our hearts' (Phil. 4:7). The Greek [*phroureo*] denotes a military word—a garrison; and so is, 'shall keep as in a garrison.' Now, a garrison has two things attending it—first, that it is exposed to the assaults of its enemies; second, that safety lies in it from their attempts. It is so with our souls; they are exposed to temptations, assaulted continually; but if there be a garrison in them, or if they be kept as in a garrison, temptation shall not enter, and consequently we shall not enter into temptation. Now, how is this done? Says he, 'The peace of God shall do it.' What is this 'peace of God'? A sense of his love and favor in Jesus Christ. Let this abide in you, and it shall garrison you against all assaults whatsoever" (204–5).

17. For additional help in writing out a temptation dialogue, we recommend Andrew A. Boa, "Facing Temptation," chap. 8 in *Redeemed Sexuality: Healing and Transformation in Community; 12 Sessions* (Downers Grove, IL: IVP Connect, 2017).

18. We got this question from David Powlison, *Making All Things New: Restoring Joy to the Sexually Broken* (Wheaton, IL: Crossway, 2017), 73.

19. We got this question from Powlison, 73.

20. C. S. Lewis, *Mere Christianity* (repr., New York: Macmillan, 1960), 124–25.

21. On this same idea, Leon Morris writes, "Many have pointed out that the Sinless One knows the force of temptation in a way that we who sin do not. We give in before the temptation has fully spent itself; only he who does not yield knows its full force." Leon Morris, *Hebrews*, in *The Expositor's Bible Commentary*, vol. 12, *Hebrews through Revelation* (Grand Rapids: Zondervan, 1981), 46.

22. See Owen, "Of Temptation," 206.

23. See Matt Fradd, *The Porn Myth: Exposing the Reality behind the Fantasy of Pornography* (San Francisco: Ignatius Press, 2017), 182.

Chapter 16: Killing or Replacing Bad Desires

1. John Freeman, *Hide or Seek: When Men Get Real with God about Sex* (Greensboro, NC: New Growth Press, 2014), 17.

2. Matt Fradd, *The Porn Myth: Exposing the Reality behind the Fantasy of Pornography* (San Francisco: Ignatius Press, 2017), 181–82.

3. See Freeman, *Hide or Seek*, 117–18.

4. Timothy Keller's paraphrase of Chalmers, from "Sowing and Reaping" (sermon, Redeemer Presbyterian Church, New York, NY, May 17, 1998), quoted in Freeman, 105. Chalmers expounds on this point elsewhere in the sermon: "There are two ways in which a practical moralist may attempt to displace from the human heart its love of the world—either by a demonstration of the world's vanity, so as that the heart shall be prevailed upon simply to withdraw its regards from an object that is not worthy of it; or, by setting forth another object, even God, as more worthy of its attachment, so as that the heart shall be prevailed upon not to resign an old affection, which shall have nothing to succeed it, but to exchange an old affection for a new one. My purpose is to show, that from the constitution of our nature, the former method is altogether incompetent and ineffectual—and that the latter method will alone suffice for the rescue and recovery of the heart from the wrong affection that domineers over it." Thomas Chalmers, *The Expulsive Power of a New Affection*, ed. William Hanna (repr., Minneapolis: Curiosmith, 2012), 7.

5. Hence, we used the term *faith-driven repentance* in repentance chapters.

Chapter 17: Recovering after a Fall

1. Wayne Grudem, *Systematic Theology: An Introduction to Biblical Doctrine* (Grand Rapids: Zondervan, 1994), 198

2. Edward T. Welch, *Addictions: A Banquet in the Grave* (Phillipsburg, NJ: P&R Publishing, 2001), 240.

Chapter 18: Understanding Guilt and Shame

1. Edward T. Welch, *Shame Interrupted: How God Lifts the Pain of Worthlessness and Rejection* (Greensboro, NC: New Growth Press, 2012), 2.

2. Richard Sibbes, "The Matchless Mercy," in *The Complete Works of Richard Sibbes*, ed. Alexander Balloch Grosart, vol. 7, *Containing Miscellaneous Sermons, Indexes, Etc.* (Edinburgh, 1864), 157, quoted in David Sunday, "How to Fight When You Fail," Desiring God, June 19, 2019, https://www .desiringgod.org/articles/how-to-fight-when-you-fail/.

3. Welch, *Shame Interrupted*, 3.

4. See Heather Davis Nelson, "Free in Christ: Performance Shame," chap. 5 in *Unashamed: Healing Our Brokenness and Finding Freedom from Shame* (Wheaton, IL: Crossway, 2016).

5. This whole subsection was helped by Joe M. Sprinkle's article "Clean, Unclean," in *Evangelical Dictionary of Biblical Theology*, ed. Walter A. Elwell (Grand Rapids: Baker Books, 1996), available online at https://www.bible studytools.com/dictionary/clean-unclean/, along with "Clean and Unclean, Holy and Common," chap. 8 in Welch, *Shame Interrupted*.

6. See Welch, *Shame Interrupted*, 131–36.

7. David Powlison, *Making All Things New: Restoring Joy to the Sexually Broken* (Wheaton, IL: Crossway, 2017), 27.

Chapter 19: Understanding and Disciplining the Body

1. See William M. Struthers, *Wired for Intimacy: How Pornography Hijacks the Male Brain* (Downers Grove, IL: IVP Books, 2009), 101.

2. Struthers, 85.

3. See Donald L. Hilton Jr., "Slave Master: How Pornography & Drugs Changes Your Brain," *Salvo*, no. 13 (Summer 2010): 5–6. Available online at https:// salvomag.com/article/salvo13/slave-master.

4. Hilton, 5.

5. Hilton, 6.

6. This doesn't excuse the lack of volitional comprehension of the consequences, but it explains the neurochemical basis for it!

7. Andrea García Cerdán, "Mirror Neurons: The Most Powerful Learning Tool," CogniFit, June 8, 2017, https://blog.cognifit.com/mirror-neurons/. What is especially useful in this article is the TED video explaining mirror neurons: Vilayanur Ramachandran, "The Neurons That Shaped Civilization," filmed November 2009 in Mumbai, India, TEDIndia video, 7:27.

8. See Struthers, *Wired for Intimacy*, 95–96.

9. Struthers, 96. See also Matt Fradd, *The Porn Myth: Exposing the Reality behind the Fantasy of Pornography* (San Francisco: Ignatius Press, 2017), 194.

10. See Edward T. Welch, *Addictions: A Banquet in the Grave* (Phillipsburg, NJ: P&R Publishing, 2001), 51–52.

11. See Fradd, *The Porn Myth*, 184.

12. Welch, *Addictions*, 51.

13. Though the exposition here of Titus 2 is ours, it was inspired by Welch, 217–18.

14. See Fradd, *The Porn Myth*, 183.

15. See Fradd, 193.

16. Fradd, 180.

17. Quoted in Fradd, 180.

Chapter 20: Getting a Glimpse of the Big Picture

1. David Powlison, "Is Sexual Renewal a Simple or Complex Process?" Crossway, August 10, 2017, https://www.crossway.org/articles/is-sexual-renewal-a-simple-or-complex-process/.

2. David Powlison, *Making All Things New: Restoring Joy to the Sexually Broken* (Wheaton, IL: Crossway, 2017), 21.

3. David Powlison, "An Open Letter to Those Debilitated by Their Sexual Sin," Crossway, August 21, 2017, https://www.crossway.org/articles/an-open-letter-to-those-debilitated-by-their-sexual-sin/.

Chapter 21: Acknowledging True Beauty

1. Alan Noble, "What I Learned about Lust and Beauty from a Flickr Voyeur," *Christ and Pop Culture* 2, no. 6 (2014), http://christandpopculture.com/learned-lust-beauty-flickr-voyeur/.

2. Leland Ryken, *The Liberated Imagination: Thinking Christianly about the Arts* (1989; repr., Eugene, OR: Wipf & Stock, 2005), 70–71.

3. Matthew Lee Anderson, *Earthen Vessels: Why Our Bodies Matter to Our Faith* (Minneapolis: Bethany House, 2011), 88–89.

4. Colby Itkowitz, "This Man Had the Most Touching Response to Seeing His Wife's Body Photoshopped," *The Washington Post*, October 16, 2015, https://www.washingtonpost.com/news/inspired-life/wp/2015/10/16/husband-to-photographer-who-airbrushed-wife-you-took-away-everything-that-makes-up-our-life/.

Chapter 22: Fighting Battle Weariness

1. David Sunday, "How to Fight When You Fail," Desiring God, June 19, 2019, https://www.desiringgod.org/articles/how-to-fight-when-you-fail.
2. This story is recounted in Bryan Chapell, *Holiness by Grace: Delighting in the Joy That Is Our Strength* (Wheaton, IL: Crossway, 2001), 136.

Conclusion: Looking Forward to a Better Day

1. David Powlison, *Making All Things New: Restoring Joy to the Sexually Broken* (Wheaton, IL: Crossway, 2017), 62.

RESOURCES FOR FIGHTING PORNOGRAPHY

FOR MEN

Challies, Tim. *Sexual Detox: A Guide for Guys Who Are Sick of Porn*. Minneapolis: Cruciform Press, 2010.

Chester, Tim. *Closing the Window: Steps to Living Porn Free*. Downers Grove, IL: IVP Books, 2010.

Croft, Brian. *Help! He's Struggling with Pornography*. Wapwallopen, PA: Shepherd Press, 2014.

Freeman, John. *Hide or Seek: When Men Get Real with God about Sex*. Greensboro, NC: New Growth Press, 2014.

Lambert, Heath. *Finally Free: Fighting for Purity with the Power of Grace*. Grand Rapids: Zondervan, 2013.

Reju, Deepak. *Pornography: Fighting for Purity*. Phillipsburg, NJ: P&R Publishing, 2018.

White, David. *Sexual Sanity for Men: Re-creating Your Mind in a Crazy Culture*. Greensboro, NC: New Growth Press, 2012.

FOR WOMEN

Coyle, Rachel. *Help! She's Struggling with Pornography*. Wapwallopen, PA: Shepherd Press, 2017.

Dykas, Ellen, ed. *Sexual Sanity for Women: Healing from Sexual and Relational Brokenness*. Greensboro, NC: New Growth Press, 2012.

Thorne, Helen. *Purity Is Possible: How to Live Free of the Fantasy Trap*. Epsom, UK: Good Book Company, 2014.

Tiede, Vicki. *When Your Husband Is Addicted to Pornography: Healing Your Wounded Heart.* Greensboro, NC: New Growth Press, 2012.

FOR HUSBANDS AND WIVES

Black, R. Nicholas. *What's Wrong with a Little Porn When You're Married?* Greensboro, NC: New Growth Press, 2017.

Solomon, Curtis. *Redeem Your Marriage: Hope for Husbands Who Have Hurt through Pornography.* Greensboro, NC: New Growth Press, 2022.

Solomon, Jenny. *Reclaim Your Marriage: Grace for Wives Who Have Been Hurt by Pornography.* Greensboro, NC: New Growth Press, 2022.

FOR SINGLES

Black, R. Nicholas. *What's Wrong with a Little Porn When You're Single?* Greensboro, NC: New Growth Press, 2012.

FOR ANYONE

Powlison, David. *Coming Clean: Breaking Pornography's Hold on You.* Greensboro, NC: New Growth Press, 2012.

———. *Making All Things New: Restoring Joy to the Sexually Broken.* Wheaton, IL: Crossway, 2017.

———. *Sexual Addiction: Freedom from Compulsive Behavior.* Greensboro, NC: New Growth Press, 2010.

Roberts, Vaughan. *The Porn Problem: Christian Compassion, Convictions and Wisdom for Today's Big Issues.* Epsom, UK: Good Book Company, 2018.

Smith, Winston T. *The Problem with Masturbation.* Greensboro, NC: New Growth Press, 2009.

FOR PARENTS OF CHILDREN AND TEENAGERS

Challies, Tim. *Help! My Kids Are Viewing Pornography*. Wapwallopen, PA: Shepherd Press, 2017.

Gilkerson, Luke. *The Talk: 7 Lessons to Introduce Your Child to Biblical Sexuality*. Self-pub., CreateSpace, 2014.

Gilkerson, Luke, and Trisha Gilkerson. *Changes: 7 Biblical Lessons to Make Sense of Puberty*. Self-pub., CreateSpace, 2015.

Jenson, Kristen. *Good Pictures Bad Pictures: Porn-Proofing Today's Young Kids*. 2nd ed. Kennewick, WA: Glen Cove Press, 2018.

Perritt, John. *Not If, But When: Preparing Our Children for Worldly Images*. Fearn, UK: CF4Kids, 2020.

FOR CHILDREN AND TEENAGERS

Holcomb, Justin S., and Lindsey A. Holcomb. *God Made All of Me: A Book to Help Children Protect Their Bodies*. Greensboro, NC: New Growth Press, 2015.

Jones, Stan, and Brenna Jones. *Facing the Facts: The Truth about Sex and You*. 3rd ed. God's Design for Sex 4. Colorado Springs: NavPress, 2019.

———. *The Story of Me: Babies, Bodies, and a Very Good God*. 3rd ed. God's Design for Sex 1. Colorado Springs: NavPress, 2019.

———. *What's the Big Deal? Why God Cares about Sex*. 3rd ed. God's Design for Sex 3. Carol Stream, IL: NavPress, 2019.

Nystrom, Carolyn. *Before I Was Born: God Knew My Name*. 3rd ed. God's Design for Sex 2. Colorado Springs: NavPress, 2019.

Ryle, J. C. *Thoughts for Young Men*. 1886. Reprint, Amityville, NY: Calvary Press, 1996.

Deepak Reju (MDiv, PhD, The Southern Baptist Theological Seminary) is pastor of the biblical counseling and family ministries at Capitol Hill Baptist Church in Washington, DC. He is the editor of the 31-Day Devotionals for Life series and the author of a number of books, including *Pornography: Fighting for Purity* and *On Guard: Preventing and Responding to Child Abuse at Church*. He serves on the Biblical Counseling Coalition's board of directors and is a trustee for the Christian Counseling & Educational Foundation (CCEF). Deepak is married to Sarah, and they have two sons and three daughters.

Jonathan D. Holmes (MA, Trinity Evangelical Divinity School) is the founder and executive director of Fieldstone Counseling and the pastor of counseling for Parkside Church Bainbridge and Green. He is the author of several books, including *Counsel for Couples: A Biblical and Practical Guide for Marriage Counseling*; a frequent speaker at conferences and retreats; and a trustee for the Christian Counseling & Educational Foundation (CCEF). Jonathan is married to Jennifer, and they have four daughters.

YOUR COMPANION IN THE
FIGHT AGAINST PORN

What makes a woman's encounter with pornography different from a man's, and how do you counsel her? What guidance do you give a struggler who is currently dating—or married? How can you help parents who have discovered that their young child has been exposed to porn? *Rescue Plan* gives concrete information and helps you to shape an effective plan of attack for strugglers in these diverse circumstances.

"An extremely practical resource, rooted in the gospel, for porn strugglers and those who want to help them to find freedom."
—**John Freeman**, Founder, Harvest USA

"A practical, biblical, and gospel-saturated guidebook . . . remarkably candid . . . saturated in gospel hope."
—**R. Albert Mohler Jr.**, President, The Southern Baptist Theological Seminary

"A comprehensive, hope-filled, and practical guide for sexual sinners regardless of gender, age, or life stage."
—**Brenda Pauken**, Biblical Counselor, Sterling Park Baptist Church, Sterling, Virginia

ALSO BY DEEPAK REJU

Is there any hope for those in the "voluntary slavery" of pornography addiction? Deepak Reju points out that this worship problem can be fought only with a greater love for Christ. This monthlong devotional, with reflection questions and practical suggestions for action, gives you the encouragement and preparation you need for the war being waged for your soul every day.

"Reju's work on pornography is relentlessly biblical, consistently practical, and wonderfully aggressive in laying out the need for godly community and humility. I have worked with many who struggled with pornography, and I wish I could have had this resource to give to each of them!"
—**Alasdair Groves**, Executive Director, Christian Counseling & Educational Foundation

"Here is medicine in the form of meditations. . . . Begin each day, for a month, with Deepak reading you and teaching you from Scripture. Plainspoken, searching, practical, humble, and hopeful—this could be just what you've been looking for in your struggle for something better than fantasy."
—**Mark Dever**, Senior Pastor, Capitol Hill Baptist Church, Washington, DC; President, 9Marks

Did you find this book helpful?
Consider leaving a review online.
The authors appreciate your feedback!

Or write to P&R at editorial@prpbooks.com
with your comments. We'd love to hear from you.